Fair Of Face
By Anne Lyken-Garner

The follow-up to 'Sunday's Child'

A nineteenth century poem

Monday's child is fair of face,

Tuesday's child is full of grace,

Wednesday's child is full of woe,

Thursday's child has far to go.

Friday's child is loving and giving,

Saturday's child works hard for a living,

And the child that is born on the Sabbath Day, is bonny and blithe and good and gay.

Fair Of Face refers to someone who's pleasing to the eye. It also describes a pleasing, positive, well-behaved child with an optimistic nature; one who conforms to an adult's idea of goodness - based on the social rules of the day.

I chose *'Sunday's Child'* as the working title of the first book because I mistakenly thought the poem said, *'Sunday's Child is full of woe.'* By the time I finished the book, I realised that the title was perfect because the story wasn't about woe. It was about inspiration and encouragement!

Naturally, the name of the sequel had to follow Sunday's Child. I didn't want to call it Monday's Child, so I went for Fair of Face.

Author's note

In 'Sunday's Child' (the first book), I allowed the action to move the story forward. I decided to adapt a different device in 'Fair Of Face' and allowed the introduction of each new *character* to move through the events, especially in the first half of the book.

'Fair Of Face' is 100% true. However, some of the events may not have happened in chronological order, as they didn't fit in well with how I wanted the story to progress. As in the first book, I've changed most of the 'characters' names, and have disguised them to avoid embarrassment on their part.

While I don't pretend to have an accurate impression of the things that happened (I could, after all, only see them from my own perspective), I want to assure you that I've worked my hardest to precisely *capture* my teenage and early twenties' thoughts and ideas.

I've been asked if I will write another book in the series and the answer is no. However, I wanted to give the reader a glimpse of my life as a 'grown-up.' I've therefore used flash-forwards (preceded by the phrase: *Please Prophet tell me what you see*) in 'Fair Of Face,' as I've had positive feedback on the flashbacks I used in Sunday's Child.

Just for fun, I've included a Guyanese proverb at the end of some of the chapters.

Dedicated to my late relatives and friends who appeared in this book:

My mum
My aunt, Theresa (she died too young)
My maternal grandmother, (nee) Elizabeth
My paternal grandmother, Elizabeth
My paternal uncle, Compton
My paternal uncle, John
My paternal aunt, Babs
My maternal uncle, Christopher
My sister, Sandra
'Razor Da Silva'
'Aunty' Sheila
Miss Hyacinth
George
TNM
'Darla'
'Leroy'

Acknowledgements

*I'm forever grateful to the following people:
Morganne Garner for the front cover image; Steve
Garner for all the encouragement, for making me
rewrite the ending, and for the suggestions and
edits; and Colleen DeLoach for editing and for
sharing my work.
I also want to thank the Guyana Gallery Facebook
group for helping me with the translation of a few of
the Guyanese proverbs.*

CHAPTER 1 – GEORGE AND THE BUZZING BEES

"Peddle faster! Yuh going too slow!" Moira shouted.

"I'm trying. *You* try riding a bike on this gravelly road with someone on the back carrier," I answered.

"Owww!" Moira groaned as we hit another crater in the road.

"Sorry. I still learning, yuh know," I said through shallow breaths.

"Anne, maybe I should tow *you* when we get round this corner. Ah been riding since I was five."

"Uh huh." I knew she was right. After all, at fifteen I'd just learned to cycle. The mechanics of the steering and rounding my legs on the pedals at the same time took me the entire summer holiday to grapple.

"What's that sound?"

"Sounds like loud buzzing," Moira answered.

During the first few weeks back from the summer holidays, Moira and I fancied going for a ride after school. She said I could use her bike to practise my cycling.

I'd used Brian's (my new friend) bike all through the holidays. We'd hung out several times a week under the priest's house, playing table tennis. And while the other players took their turn ping-ponging, Brian took me – and his bike out into the street and steadied the back of the seat like a doting dad.

He guided me while I awkwardly convulsed myself left to right, then onto the hot, bruising tarmac several times each day. He picked me up, helped me get back on his bike, and off I went again, heaving from side to side. I'd made it through worse than hot bruises before. To me, they were just peanuts.

It occurred to Moira and me within a split second of each other, that we were going past a flower garden, and the sound we heard wasn't *like* buzzing it *was* buzzing.

"Peddle faster, Anne!" she shouted again.
I puffed the air even harder, but within an instant, sharp, hot needles attacked my exposed hands on the handlebars.

Forgetting I was cycling, I instinctively drew them up to my face, which, for the second time in my life was buzzing with a swarm of angry bees. Moira and I crashed to the gravel-and-stone-covered road, and merged into the bike.

The bees didn't seem too interested in us once they'd stung us. When we surveyed the damage on our bodies, we were blanketed in raw, bleeding cuts and bruises from the fall. My elbows and knees were skin-less, and so were the insides of both my hands.

Moira was far luckier than I was. She was sitting on the carrier, which was much nearer to the ground. *And* she'd had more than a decade's worth of practice jumping off falling bikes. At least I wouldn't wake up with a balloon face tomorrow morning, because *I'd* had practice with bee stings.

We got off the ground, dusted each other off and Moira towed me home. As she did, I thought about the first time I spoke to her.

We didn't officially meet each other until our fourth year in high school. She was sitting in front of me in class. One day while we were having a conversation she told me there was a scar in the shape of a heart on my forehead.

As I couldn't remember how it got there, she'd said at the time that an angel must've sneaked into our house one night and branded me.

I limped into the yard, already stiff with excruciating pain by the time I got home. I didn't ask Moira – *or* anyone else in. They couldn't know there was no adult living with me.

One of our three yard neighbours, Sasha saw me first. She took one look at my bloody injuries and waved her hands in the air – shrieking. She hollered for George next door, and he came racing down the stairs, generous belly, jellying up and down.

I sat in the yard, on the very last step of Uncle's stairs and they both surveyed my injuries. George said he had something upstairs that would help and limped off to go get it.

As soon as I told Sasha about how I fell, she burst out laughing.

"So yuh trying to beat bees off yuh face while riding a bike?"

"Yeah."

"So which hand were yuh usin' for steadying the bike on that rocky road?"

"Ah wasn't thinking straight, was I?"

"Did you fall on the bike or did it fall on you?" Sasha chuckled.

"Well, both sort of . . . like kinda into each other."

"How yuh mean?" Sasha was almost screaming with laughter, her short, straight, boyish hair trumpeting in the wind. Surprisingly, I couldn't help giggling either. We were still laughing when George returned with something hidden behind his back.

"What you got?" I asked my neighbour. He was the housemate of our septuagenarian landlady, Miss Hyacinth. When George was sober and wasn't going off to see his estranged family across the river, he boarded in the living room of her one-bedroom house.

When he *wasn't* sober – which was several times a week, the grey-haired, fat and balding George had to sleep on her veranda. We saw him first-thing when we emerged from Miss Hyacinth's downstairs, garage-like room she rented us.

George didn't seem to mind sleeping outdoors. His friends and his rum mattered to him more than Miss Hyacinth's nagging.

Sasha went over to George and yelped at what she saw hidden behind his back. He wasn't a tall man, but beside him, Sasha looked like a little girl.

"You sure that gon help?" she asked him.

"Yeah, mon. This is me good stuff," he answered.

George and Sasha sort of took care of me in their own weird way. Sasha was years older than me, and had a baby of her own. In the absence of a responsible adult in my home, *she* was the one whose house I went to for food when I was hungry.

A man who sometimes spent the night passed-out in the ditch outside our yard wasn't someone I'd let 'doctor' me unless I knew what he was holding.

"Whatever yuh got there, George, yuh better not get close to me with it." I got up and limped away, knees almost completely stiff.

"Is dis, mon," he told me, holding out a wide-mouthed bottle of methylated spirits. I knew that purple thing well. My grandmother always had a supply of it in a special little bottle.

"Yuh sure that ain't the one you drink from, George?" Sasha asked, laughing. "I don't want yuh to poison the child."

"I don't drink this, Sash!" George looked indignant, but he knew that *we* knew he was lying. "You hold she down, and I gon pour it on."

"You guys, am freaking out here," I said, but no one was paying attention to me. "That thing burns like hell."

Big George stood in our yard, opposite little Sasha, the two carrying on a conversation about me that didn't include me.

I was the youngest person living in the yard *apart* from baby Ella in the front house, Sasha's own toddler, and my little sister. Baby Ella lived with her mum Donna, who was waiting for her husband to come back from Canada and take her and their child to live in luxury with him there.

Donna shared the large house with her baby and her sister-in-law Elaine, whose father owned that house and the land on which the other two houses stood.

Sasha was in the same boat. She lived in the middle house owned by her boyfriend's uncle (who we called 'Uncle'), with her baby, Jay. *Her* boyfriend was coming back from the U.S one day to sweep her off her feet once more.

"Look at me, George," Sasha said, palms outward and open at her sides. "I is half her height. Yuh think she will let me hold her down?"

"Alright, I'll sit down." I gave in, not wanting to be held down in the public yard, in view of all the nosy neighbours on both sides of the fallen chicken-wire fence.

"But put a small bit on first and if it hurts, you guys have to stop, right?"

"Sure," George said and approached me with his half-drunk mentholated spirits. "Bring a piece a' cloth, Sash. Ah gon jus daub on a little."

I half turned to look at Sasha, but from the corner of my eye, I saw George lift his hand and throw something in my direction. Before I could lift my bottom off the step, the remains of the purple stuff was drizzling down my raw knees and shins.

I screamed, flew off the step and did a head-less chicken dance around the yard. Sasha and George screamed with laughter, and to be honest, so did I when the burning cooled.

I suppose it was pretty funny if you were sitting on Miss Hyacinth's step watching a teenaged girl hop around a large genip tree, screaming her head off. If she was accompanied by a tiny five-foot tall woman bursting her guts laughing, and an overweight man in his early sixties wearing nothing but a pair of too-small shorts, guffawing so loudly, the long scar on the side of his pregnant belly seam to split open once again, it would be funnier still.

Caught in the middle of my electric pain and crippling laughter, I understood – looking at George – what side-splitting laughter really meant.

"Ah only helping yuh, Anne," George said, tears of laughter streaming down his face. "Gotta give it to yuh, though," he gasped between breaths. "Yuh got a high pain threshold. I not going to sit there and let no one put meths on me bruises. At least it will kill them germs."

As I limped indoors into the storeroom enclosure below Miss Hyacinth's house where we lived, still seething from the pain, I heard Sasha say, "Hey, George, where ever you end up tonight, don't go near hospital street."

"Yuh say '*tonight.*' You know the 'boss lady' doan let me in if ah turn up after nine o' clock," George replied – his voice low, obviously referring to the nightly heated discussions he and Miss Hyacinth had when he knocked on her door after she'd gone to bed.

Miss Hyacinth preferred to fret loudly in her bed, rather than wake up to open the door and let him in. Living in her storeroom, right under her bedroom, her voice was like the cricket chirps – one of our usual night time noises.

CHAPTER 2 – MISS HYACINTH AND HER KITCHEN SHOP

We met George, Sasha and Miss Hyacinth on the day we left my grandmother. I had no idea where we were packing to go to, but from my vast experience in moving, I thought we were going to another house on our own.

I was surprised when I realised we were moving half our stuff (my grandmother was left with the other half) into an elderly lady's living room.

My aunt Theresa and Miss Hyacinth had worked for the same rich people in town. Theresa was their maid and cook, and Miss Hyacinth – well-known around town as 'Iron Lady' – was, well, their . . . iron lady.

The look on her face as we moved in our half-broken household stuff told me that *wasn't* what she was expecting.

At seventy-eight years old, Miss Hyacinth raised chickens, took in ironing, and worked as a cleaner in the opposition party's office in town. She also ran a successful business from her home, selling dry goods in small quantities – both for cash and on credit.

Her house was not ten minutes from my school. The longer we lived in her storeroom, the more amazed I was that she agreed to take us in because of how private she was. Her front steps were accessible, but the back ones were fenced in so that access to her 'bottom house' was only *through* her house.

The morning after the move, once we got up off the living room floor, my six-year-old sister, Franc, my young aunt, Theresa and I walked downstairs to look around.

Enclosed under the front third of Miss Hyacinth's house, inside her secure barbed wire fence, was a small room with one naked light bulb hanging from the ceiling. The room was about eleven foot long by eight foot wide, divided down the middle by a shoulder-high sheet of plywood.

The middle third of Miss Hyacinth's bottom house was a passageway leading to the side of her property, where she had an outside bathroom and a washing line. (She had an indoor bathroom but was raising little chicks in it – little ones that couldn't yet go out to the big pen). This passageway also led to a lean-to shed, which had a fire-side in it.

The final third of Miss Hyacinth's bottom house was an enormous chicken pen, locked with two separate padlocks, where we were never allowed to go.

The storeroom became our home at my suggestion. Miss Hyacinth agreed to rent it to us and by the end of the day we were living in it.

The occupants of the middle house where Sasha lived, and those of Miss Hyacinth's house used the latrine at the back of the property. Miss Hyacinth reserved her indoor toilet for 'laying' chickens.

Her kitchen was the strangest I'd ever seen. Most of it was overrun by old plastic bags, weighing scales, and plastic vats of foodstuff like onions, milk powder, sugar, rice, and salt. After her workday, her kitchen corner-shop became alive.

The loose food she sold was convenient to starving families because she was prepared to sell them in the smallest possible portions.

But not only this, she gave credit to her customers, which was obvious from all the chalk coloured writing on her kitchen wall. Every clear wall space was decorated with names of people, with even more figures and totals under them.

This week 'Boyo' had bought one egg, one single cigarette, and four tablespoons of salt on credit.

'Geeta' picked up two eddoes, a cup of rice, a cup of kerosene oil and three spoons of curry powder. 'Geeta' was obviously making a meal for one.

It wasn't surprising that the people who had the longest list were those who bought the smallest amounts of stuff.

I looked at some of the figures the first morning we'd woken up on her floor, and for the first time in my life realised that you spent a lot more by buying things in small quantities. I'd always thought the opposite was true.

I guess that meant that poor people like us spent a lot more than richer people – only because we couldn't afford to buy bigger quantities in the first place. Is that the way the world worked? Did you spend more because you had less?

Miss Hyacinth didn't sell perishables. She said she couldn't afford to.

When her stock of rice got infested with weevils, she picked them out and sold the rice anyway. But at least she made an effort. The market sellers left the de-weeviling to their *customers*.

Miss Hyacinth never sold her chickens – ever. They were 'working' chickens she'd said. As she went on talking about her employed fowls, I drifted off, imagining child-sized chickens wearing hair-nets and aprons serving in cafes. In my mind they tucked their tips under their wings and clucked their thanks to their customers.

Chef chickens were in the kitchen, slaving away in front of the stoves, which they had to stand on step-ladders to use. One of my imagined chicks caught her tail feather in the flame as she turned away from her pot, and clucked wildly for her colleagues to come over and fan her out.

Miss Hyacinth kept her chicks for the profit she could get from selling their eggs. Even her lame, bald hens were still profitable. When they died from old age, Miss Hyacinth cut their necks and curried them. Otherwise, she didn't eat chicken.

"Ah used to sell potatoes and flour, girl," she told me one day. "And yuh can get a lot a profit with things like them. That Burnham tek everything away from people."

"Yes, Miss Hyacinth," I said, hoping she would just go and get the two cigarettes I had come to get for my mum.

Miss Hyacinth's favourite complaint was about Burnham and the ruling P.N.C party. She'd been a part of the main opposition political party all her life. "Unusual for a black woman like me," she'd said.

"Ah went to visit me cousin in the hospital yesterday," she had continued. "Girl yuh won't believe the smell. All de blackouts we had last week mek all them dead bodies at the mortuary rot down to nothing. Again!"

Miss Hyacinth still hadn't moved. Her face had long since lost its blackness. It had a smooth greyness to it, which reminded me of my grandmother's. I bet her skin wasn't cold like my grandmother's. I'd never touched her, but couldn't help noting the similarity of the old, grey, almost wrinkle-less skin.

Maybe Miss Hyacinth was just lonely. Why else would she talk to *me*? I was sure I didn't *look* very interested.

I'd heard about the blackout mortuary thing. Everyone had been avoiding the hospital and the entire area recently because of it. Just like lining up for food, bread and kerosene oil (never fully expecting to get any), blackouts were a norm.

At last Miss Hyacinth had slowly begun to move away, hunched over slightly like someone just about to get up off a couch. Her ironing hand hung a bit lower than the other – thumb poised slightly at right angles to her hand.

She dragged one foot behind her, making the swift sifting sound we'd grown accustomed to hearing early in the morning. She went to bed promptly at the same time every night – a few minutes past nine o'clock, just after listening to the death announcements on the radio.

Every night this ritual seemed to convince her that she was still going strong, as one by one the big, fat eraser called death was scrubbing out the names she knew at school.

CHAPTER 3 – AARAN

After we'd settled in our new little home, my mum decided it was time for her leave the country again to return to work in the bar – just like she'd done for years.

"But ah thought you wasn't going back at all," Theresa had said to her. "Isn't that what this move was about?"

"I thought so too, but ah think I should make *one* more trip," Mum had replied. "We need money, don't we?"

"Yeah, but yuh can find all sorts of work right here, can't yuh?"

"Is only one last trip," my mother said. "Tell you what, I won't go all the way to French Guiana like I did before. I'll just go to Suriname. Ah know the Palentaks there and can get work in their bar. I used to work there when Anne was littler, remember?"

"Okay, then," my aunt Theresa had agreed. "Me and the girls will be alright." (Or so she thought).

"I know. Yuh took care of them all their lives anyway. This wouldn't be different from normal."

My little sister, Franc and I weren't really happy about our mum going away. We always thought – naturally, that once we left our grandmother's prison, we'd live happily ever after with our mother and get to know her.

We didn't have a say in the matter, though. After all, we were just kids and she was going to work to get money for *us*.

Mum said we would get credit from Miss Hyacinth and that she would pay her when she got back. She said that the little money Theresa was earning as a domestic should be fine for us in the meantime.

Two days after mum left, Theresa had her third nervous breakdown and had to go into the mental hospital.

I went to bed a child and work up an adult. And when they told me that unaccompanied children weren't allowed into the asylum, it didn't make any sense that they wouldn't let *me* in.

Between getting me and my six-year-old sister to school, cooking in the lean-to on the fire-side, cleaning and trying to find food, there wasn't much time left to do anything else.

Eventually, after two weeks – even with the limited dry foods we could possibly get from her, we had run up our credit limit on Miss Hyacinth's kitchen wall.

I was so wrong thinking I could pull it off by holding on and pretending it was all going to go away.

***

Aaran and I were inseparable – she's the first friend I thought of as my sister. Last summer we spent every day with each other, playing table tennis, walking around town, or just listening to the radio at my house.

At lunchtime, about three times a week, she bought us meals at one of the best Chinese restaurants in town, which just happened to be at the top of the street where she lives.

This luxury came at a price, though. Aaran warned me that we had to hide if we ever saw her mother while eating out. Aaran's father secretly gave her extra pocket money in addition to the amount her mother was giving her. She would be in a pickle if her mum ever found out.

Ever since my mother and aunt left, Aaran has come to our house for a smoke – that is, if she managed to get hold of her dad's cigarette box.

"Ah don't understand why yuh won't smoke, Anne. No one here to see us," she said, lying next to me on the bed, with one arm across her forehead, puffing smoke up to the ceiling. She seemed at peace with the world and the serene puffs of smoke rising up to the unpainted wooden boards above our heads.

"It's not that, is it?" I answered, turning sideways to face her. "Ah here by meself *all the time*, but will never take up smoking. It's just not me."

But I didn't tell her of the chain-link fence and the night-guard's deliberate touch on my fingers. She would hurt too much for me. She'd want to go find him and tell him what's for. Aaran never took anything lying down.

"Never? Ah mean no one knows what'll happen in the future." Aaran puffed out another lungful of smoke. "Yuh might have a hard life or yuh might marry a man who smokes. Things happen, Anne."

"Ah know things happen, Aaran. But yuh got to decide where you want yuh life to go when yuh have the time to think. If yuh wait till yuh weak and weary, you'll obviously take the easy way out. Besides, if a hard life made a person smoke, *you* wouldn't be doing it right now."

"Shush you!" Aaran threw a pillow at me. "I just having some fun and you would too if yuh try it. Yuh know, Anne if ah didn't know better, I'd say you were thirty, not fifteen."

Of course, Aaran was right. I didn't really know how to have fun. It would probably take years for me to learn.

"Things happen," I answered. "Ah had to grow up. Besides, yuh know I tried it. The first time yuh came here with them, ah tried one with yuh, remember?"

Aaran laughed her hearty, belly laugh. Her eyes squeezed shut and her long, luxurious eyebrows shadowed her cheeks. Against her fair skin, her dark hair stood out like an artist's heavily-pencilled outline on a portrait.

Her laughter seemed to come from somewhere deep inside her soul – somewhere where lots of laughter was stored up, ready to bubble up to the surface and spring forth.

"Yeah, but yuh just took one puff. That's not really trying something, is it?" Aaran asked. "Ah been trying them for a while. Ah didn't like them at first either, but now, man, these are so relaxing."

"That's just the point, girl. Ah don't *want* to like them.

She had hit the nail on the head as they say. My reason for not wanting to try more than a couple of puffs is I *didn't* want to give myself any reason to like cigarettes.

I didn't want to be like my grandmother. I didn't want to do anything she did.

Being like her involves an open-sore situation that I had experienced first-hand. It was the constant, painful eating away of flesh I was still fighting to survive and overcome.

Today was the last day of the first term of school. It was to be the beginning of the Christmas holidays. I hoped that Mum would be back soon so we could spend Christmas together.

Once in a while I get a call from Sasha next door. She presents me a plate of food she says she had 'left over'. She tells me she's cooked 'too much' but I know what she means.

"Anne, there's someone at the door." Aaran said to me, bringing me out of my daydream. She quickly stubbed her cigarette out on the front the box she brought them in. I got off the bed and looked out over the plywood that divided the room in half. We had only one tiny wooden window, so our two wooden doors stayed open.

The uniform the man at our front door was wearing looked very familiar to me.

"Yes?" I asked, leaving Aaran behind the partition wall we called our bedroom and coming around to see him.

"Yuh mother home, girl?"

"No, she's at the shop," I lied.

"What time's she coming back?"

"Doan know."

"Well I have to serve these papers to you. I got legal business," he said, signalling the two men who were waiting a long way away. He handed me a typewritten sheet of paper.

"Can I ask that you read this?" he said when it was in my hands.

"Yuh done?" he asked after I handed the paper back to him. My hands were dancing wildly to the drumbeat inside my chest.

"Hmmm. Wha . . . what's this? Who's Mrs. Jainaught?" I was confused, as panic pounded like a hammer on the side of my head.

"Your mother knows who she is. She owes her hundreds of dollars for goods she took from her market stall."

Mrs. Jainaught was Shop Lady! We'd called her Shop Lady for so long, I'd forgotten what her real name was.

"I have to tell you that now we must remove all your furniture until this debt is paid."

Our years of credit had finally caught up with us.

"My mother's not really at the shops, Mister," I confessed, hoping for some kind of reprieve. "She's out of the country. Can't this wait till she comes back?"

"Oh, she's out of the country, is she?" he said, indicating for the men – who by now had walked up a bit nearer to enter the house.

Aaran had crept up behind me without me hearing. I smelt the cigarette smoke on her before I felt her arm on my shoulder.

"Yuh can't take stuff off a child, you moron. Yuh got to wait till there's an adult here!"

"I got my work to do, girl. Please step out of the house. Who're you anyway?" he asked.

"This ain't right!" Aaran insisted.

"Can yuh both step out of the house?" the man dressed in black and white said. His words brought back memories of my childhood like a swift flood of cold water.

Just like that, I was a helpless child again, desperately trying to wriggle my way out from beneath a heavy, adult world.

Today's bailiff was a lot younger than the one I met years ago – the one who refused to let me into the house I once lived in, and brought my doll naked and upside down from the long flight of stairs.

Today's official was equally threatening. Aaran and I walked out of the house, stood by the back steps of the front house where Elaine lived, and watched the men empty the house.

My sore, fragile heart broke again, flooding its misery though my eyes. I pleaded with him to wait, something I had wanted to do when I first saw that other bailiff about five years ago – but hadn't dared.

I've always wondered if I had the courage to do that then, would he have left us alone?

I was crying for all those years when I wasted thought after thought, thinking it would've made a difference.

"Doan worry," Aaran kept saying. "Doan worry."

But Aaran didn't know very much about the past I kept hidden, too embarrassed to share.

For a moment the bailiff looked a bit unsure – slightly bothered by my tears, and I almost willed him to change his mind, but as the men kept going in and out of the house, I realised that wasn't going to happen.

All he said was, "All this stuff so old. I have to take *everything* to cover the amount."

After what seemed like an entire day, we were allowed to go back inside. I noticed that they had left the little one-burner kerosene stove.

I also had two pillows. I picked one up, buried my face in it and wept for the first time of many times to come.

I'd told no one but my close friends that my mum was out of the country. I even pretended to Miss Hyacinth that my mum had just stepped out and had sent me for this or that. It was at this precise moment of my life that my brain and my mind – and even my heart aged ten years.

A Guyanese Proverb: Turtle kyaan waak if he na put he head outa he shell.

Translation: A turtle cannot walk if he doesn't put his head out of his shell.

Meaning: If something is worth doing, you'll have to take risks to do it.

CHAPTER 4 – LEROY, JERRY SAUNDERS, AND MISS BESSY

Leroy, in all his colours, lived on the other side of the street opposite Elaine's house (at the front of our yard).

They say you shouldn't trust a cook who's skinny. If this is true, Leroy was the most trustworthy cook I knew, especially when he was wearing his cut-off jeans.

Leroy was said to be the only road-side cook who, by the whizz of his fingers could whip up a cow's face, ears and hooves into the best tasting souse in town.

People came from outlying villages just to buy his food. The waiting crowd standing on the side of the road where Leroy set up his stall at four o'clock on weekdays and Saturdays were like addicts waiting for a fix.

It would be understandable if someone bit off his own finger because it got a bit entangled with Leroy's souse. The doctors, who'd *also* probably tasted Leroy's cooking, would no doubt nod their heads in empathy while sewing the digit back on.

For the handful of times my mum had bought food from him, I was still licking my fingers hours after I had eaten, just to make sure I hadn't missed one bit.

The invasion of Leroy's stall was usually over well inside of half an hour. It was a fine payback for the cooking he did in his lean-to all day.

Leroy lived in the bottom flat of his house and rented the top flat to Jerry Saunders – one of a ring of grown men who scoured the town for young girls to 'break in' and boast about.

After work, Jerry Saunders rides around town on his hunt. His run-down Yamaha bike in the small town was probably the equivalent of a convertible sports car in a *Mills and Boon* romance novel.

Saunders' game was simple; find a girl walking on her own – or with a friend. Pull up beside them and talk to either one who would listen. If the discussion is heading nowhere, jump back on the bike, say goodbye, and look for another victim.

His vigil at his window every morning as I went to Mass was therefore no surprise. He'd call out and say the sort of things he said to all his *potential* ladies.

Each day I listened to him and wondered how attractive a little girl in her school uniform could look to a man who was nearly forty. But he was always there when I got back, and again when I walked by to go to school.

My friends at school said he was a predator – just like his six other professional buddies who made up his group.

Daily, I reminded myself that a ride on his bike wouldn't make me special. I was worth much more than a ride on a stupid, black bike. *I* was going to be good – as good as Jerry Saunders was bad. *So far, I had no idea just how bad he was. But I would find out.*

The smell of Leroy's cooking tickled my nostrils as I passed his house after school. Saliva rushed to my mouth and I had to swallow in haste. I was dying for something to eat. Teddy, a young boy who helped Leroy chop up onions, light the fireside and run to the shop, was strolling out of the yard.

"Man, ah got a really bad tummy today," he said, as though we were continuing a conversation we'd started hours ago.

"Is that why yuh out of school?" I asked.

"Na mon, I don't go to school no more. They can't teach me nothing I don't already know."

"So yuh parents just let yuh drop out?" I asked him. He went to the Community High where my Uncle Christopher attended for a short time.

"They can't tell me nothing, mon, especially when my time 'o the month come around."

"What d'ya mean?" I asked swallowing gulps of laughter. I knew he thought he was a girl but this was crazy talk.

"Ah don't care what *you* think, Miss hoity-toity-I-don't-talk-to-nobody. Ah get me periods regular," Teddy said with a flip of his wrist.

Teddy probably had springs instead of bones in his wrists. Man, they worked over-time!

"I got me pads on. Wanna see?"

"No!" I screamed. "I believe you."

By this time I'd reached the entrance to my yard so I touched him on the arm and turned to walk away. I had to make a quick escape before the laughter came bursting out from inside me.

"Yuh know, you kinda not so bad," he said.

"What d'ya mean?" I said for the second time.

"Miss Bessy's children over there," Teddy said, indicating (with his head) our neighbours on the other side of the broken chicken wire fence. "They said that you B.H.S girls too hoity toity and that you never talk to no one in the street, coz you don't want to mix with we. But you not so bad. You have a gaff with me."

Teddy pranced away, wriggling his hips, which today were clad in a blue skirt. Up until last week when I first saw him in that skirt, I had never seen any of the handful of gay men in town in women's clothes.

I *did* talk to people in the street. I said hello, especially to the grown-ups. I just wasn't friends with anyone. The biggest reason was because no one – apart from Jerry Saunders, tried to make friends with *me*.

Maybe the *real* reason I wasn't friends with anyone was because I was scared that my life would turn out like theirs and I desperately didn't want it to.

If it did, then I would've failed the life that's planned 'somewhere out there' for me – the life I've known was there since I was beaten and thrashed about when I was little.

To be honest, sometimes I *did* like the street very much, and part of that was because there was so much to laugh at. I wondered why, when you could laugh at other people's lives, it was easier to forget what yours was like.

I was also scared of some of the people in my street because of the way many of them behaved. Take Miss Bessy, the woman in the neighbouring yard. She lived in a house where she never dwelled.

There were two houses in her yard – one in the front, where a nurse and her three children lived, and Miss Bessy's house in the back. Because she was obese, Miss Bessy had to dwell, cook and sleep in her shed at the back of her house. She had nine grown-up children and numerous grandchildren.

Most of her kids had children by various other people, who all lived in the two-bedroom house.

Miss Bessy did all the cooking. The grandchildren brought everything she needed. And when she shouted from the shed, "All yuh bring the onions!" a grand-child (or one of her children) ran from the house to the shed with the onions in hand.

"All yuh, ah say, all yuh bring them blasted matches!" she would shout later; apparently, ticked off that someone didn't think of bringing the matches when they ran the onions to her earlier. Perhaps her anger came from the fact that they only ever had one box of matches and the lay-around sons always took them into the house to smoke their ciggies. This went on all day long.

We always knew when it was time for Miss Bessy to take a wash. Because she was so overweight, and stayed in one place, she had to have a bowl of water and a small towel brought to her. She cleaned herself bit by bit, and dried herself in patches. Sometimes she would call out to no one in particular, "Yuh hafta do me back!"

Someone would emerge from the house, running downstairs cursing and almost spitting with rage but they would do it anyway.

Well, there was nothing else to do. No one went to work or anything, apart from her husband and one of her sons. One of them had started a rumour in the street that he was going out with me.

I wonder, will I ever be called to do her back, or other body parts? I'll have to get back to you on that.

Please, Prophet tell me what you see.

"Here she is," the midwife says in her musical Cork accent. She lays her tiny, soft, silky body on my chest.

"I'll leave you three to bond and I'll be back for baby in two minutes, so."

When I was told at the antenatal class that the naked new born was put on your bare chest for a couple of minutes to aid the separation process, I had no idea what an almost out-of-body experience it would be.

I feel empty – hollow down in my stomach, as if the echo of a drill has left an un-filled hole there. My body is suddenly different – minus the tiny baby I'd just pushed out of it.

Deep in my subconscious, somewhere perhaps even I don't know how to access, I feel a tinge of panic, but this doesn't compare with the joy and exhilaration I feel about the little girl who's now beginning to wriggle on my chest.

I put my hand on her back and it almost covers her entire body.

I look down at her luscious, jet-black hair. Every strand of it stands up straight as if someone rubbed an inflated balloon on her head.

The eighteen hours of pain is all forgotten. The two of us count her fingers and toes and look at her face, amazed at what we had made.

"I'll take baby now," the nurse says, and stretches out her arms.

When she comes back swaddled in blue, we gaze at our daughter's face. She has soft eyebrows and very long eyelashes – jet black. Her little cherry mouth pouts a little, and her eyes when she opens them – blue. She's the most perfect and beautiful creature on earth!

"Are you okay to try feeding her now?" The nurse asks.

"I'll try," I answer, my voice shaky.

"Don't worry," she says, "You'll be grand."

They move us out of the labour room and another couple come in. I feed Daniele, our firstborn, and I can hear her breathing – her little breaths coming in tiny, quick puffs. Then I throw up all over her.

It's midnight. My husband has missed dinner and maybe lunch as well. He's gone out into the cold, wet Irish December night, to find something to eat.

I continue to listen to her breathing as she feeds, and I know that He who has put this breath inside her will keep her safe.

CHAPTER 5 – THE KNIGHTS FAMILY

Although I didn't know it then, the solution to keeping my sister safe and fed started in the summer holidays and the best time I've ever had in my life – just after being released from my grandmother's kennel.

We'd moved at the start of the summer school holidays. Around that time I began spending a lot of time at church. After Mass each morning, I went home to have breakfast. After cleaning up our room, and carrying the day's drinking and washing water from the pipe at the front house, I went back to hang out under the priest's house. I spent hours playing ping-pong with Aaran and all the other new friends I'd made.

When my mum left, Aaran was one of the few people who knew my sister Franc and I were on our own.

She brought food items from her house to mine and we'd cook up whatever she'd managed to grab from her mother's pantry that day.

In an area where most of the kids were thin, sunburnt and already paired up with their own best friends, a skinny, outcast, poor mongrel and a rich, bold white-skinned girl made quite an odd team.

Dave was always there too. Aaran was fixated with him and the way he made us laugh, but he was always worried about what her wealthy family would say if he went out with her. He never found his voice in her presence.

I believed mum when she said there was a hierarchy in the church. She remembers a time when the rich, who could buy their pews, sat at the front – close to the priest, while their black servants stood at the back.

This is why *I* never confessed the crush I had on Aaran's older uncle, Merrick. I wouldn't fit in with Merrick's sister and her friends. There was however, a family in the church who was worse off than me. No one befriended them because they had some facial disfigurement in the form of small black lumps.

The only time I'd seen anything similar to their affliction was when I was about six years old, and my grandmother had a gentleman caller. This was during her short phase of 'looking for a boyfriend' when her friends were putting her in touch with suitable, *available* men.

It's the custom that the courting gentleman in question calls upon the lady at her home to introduce himself to her and her family.

The man who showed up on our doorstep was average height and a good bit shorter than my tall, erect grandmother. He was terribly thin, but made up for it with extremely neat hair, parted on one side.

I don't know if it was because of the look my grandmother gave him, but he was nervous and wide-eyed. The most striking thing about him was the large serving of black spots, like raised pimples covering his cheeks. I spent the hour trying not to stare at his face by doing just that.

Years later – this summer, just after our big move, I met two young girls at church. They, the Knights family, had suitor man's face marks in exactly the same spot he did.

The Knights' girls weren't popular. No one, let alone the high-flyers and front-seaters in the parish wanted to sit near them. There was even a rumour the marks were catching if you touched them.

I became quite close with the girls and was invited to their home.

"So you is the Anne I hear so much about," their mother, Agnes said to me when we met. She was surprisingly young-looking, as she stretched her neck to look at me in the face.

I nodded my head.

She led me carefully through the front room, over gaping holes in the floor, and into the kitchen.

"The girls never shut up about you. Ah wanna thank yuh for being so kind to me daughters," Agnes continued. "Nobody want to be friends with them coz everyone say they got leper."

I thought of the contagion warnings I got from some of the other teenagers and must have blushed a little.

"I embarrassing yuh?" Agnes asked.

I nodded but she continued anyway.

"It's not me, yuh know. Is they father they get it from," Agnes said, as she stroked her own smooth cheeks to demonstrate. "Me two children from me previous husband look good. Is only these four look like this. Me and you, we not frighten to catch leper."

"Shut up, Mammy," Nita the oldest said quietly, but her mother's lips trembled as she continued anyway.

"Ah never realised people would be so cruel to me children – even the people at the church. They not so cruel to little Eric 'cos he a'int got the things on he face."

"Daddy coming!" Marcia (the second daughter) said from the front window. Theirs was a rusty, decapitated house overlooking a majestic church.

We heard their dad come up the stairs, then tread lightly as he stepped on the soft, bouncy boards and over the holes in the living room floor.

Like years before, in my other life altogether, I saw the skinny man of average height, wearing extremely neat hair, parted on one side. As he stepped into the kitchen where we were, the sun dipped outside the bare glass window and cast a shadow on his face. The spots looked darker and larger than I remembered them.

I recognised him instantly, but was sure he didn't know who I was.

Before I left his house I had worked out that when he came calling on my grandmother all those years ago, he'd already had Nita and the two other daughters.

I decided that their dad's secret would also be mine. After all, how would I begin to tell the girls his story, and what would I say?

From that afternoon, I went to pick the girls up so we outcasts could arrive at the ping-pong table under Father's house together.

***

When my mother went away and my aunt went into hospital, I had to find somewhere safe to leave my little sister.

I also had to find a way to stay in school and stay straight. I needed a couple of days to think.

I told the Knights of my confusion, and before I could ask, they offered to keep my sister temporarily. *They* were a family with a proper mum and a proper dad, and a loving, happy home – a home broken in every way *apart* from the people in it.

They sent her to school every day with their own son who happened to be her age – and went to the same school. She was happy and always had food. Most importantly, she had two grown-ups to take care of her if something went wrong – not a fifteen-year-old sister who didn't know where her next meal was coming from.

Each day when I came to morning Mass with the handful of older people who attended, I popped over to see how she was doing before going home and having whatever breakfast I'd manage to scavenge the day before.

Our house was now completely empty, save for the stove and the bed. I hid it the best I could from visitors who came calling. Aaran was probably the only person who knew about the bailiff. I lied to everyone else about where the few pieces of furniture we had were gone.

CHAPTER 6 – NAVIN

Our street was one of the most well-known around town. Ordinary townspeople never walked through it unless they lived there. If you thought you were tough enough, you may have ventured to visit someone in it.

Nearby lay the rich, posh area where the elite of the town and foreigners lived.

Despite having those classy areas on its doorstep, our street was the worst one in the town. It was the prostitutes' main pick up area because most of them lived there.

Our yard bordered a bigger yard of tiny squatting huts, occupied mainly by 'night girls' who spent much of their days sleeping or getting reading for 'work.'

The huts were on both sides of the street – about ten on each side. We heard the girls' carrying-ons, their babies screaming, and their lavish swearing during the day and in the early evening.

I wondered why the prostitutes lived in such awful accommodation when they made so much money going up to Bermine to the foreign sailors. I wondered what they spent it all on.

Navin was a charming little boy who lived in one of the huts. He sometimes strayed into our yard to talk with Sasha and me. On blackout nights, he stayed until after nine.

Miss Hyacinth throws her voice down if she hears us talking past her bedtime. We sit outside, under the big genip tree and listen out for the death-announcement theme on the radio around nine o' clock (which we could clearly hear from outside her wooden house). After the final note is played, and we hear the last of her dragging feet, we turn down our voice volumes.

At this time of night, the front part of the street is slowly going to sleep. By the time the crickets' chirping have fully kicked in to fill the dark, starry night, the hut girls have gone in their taxis to the ships, Miss Bessy's brood are upstairs smoking and arguing in the house, and *she* has settled in her shed. Uncle has also gone out on his night-shift work at the Electricity Company (Sasha jokes that he goes to turn the switches off).

Seven-year-old Navin walks with a limp, and has five younger brothers and sisters. The left side of Navin's body hasn't worked since he was a toddler, so his parents have never sent him to school. This neglect isn't surprising when you consider that he wasn't born disabled.

When he was still a baby his parents separated. Because his mother was a conventional Indian girl who'd hardly been to school, there wasn't much she could do with her life.

Like my old friend, Roma, Navin's mum was supposed to learn to be a good wife for her future husband. This meant that school was not important past the age of thirteen or so.

She knew how to cook and clean well and knew better than to leave the husband she would one day marry. Serving him and his parents was important. It's what an honest, traditional girl would do.

In return, her husband's parents would give her a roof to live under, and clothes to put on her back. The problem with this is that when your husband's family throws you out of their house, you have nothing left but destitution.

And if you had your family to fall back on, it may not be so bad for you and your baby. However, the mere existence of said baby – minus daddy becomes a disgrace to the girl's family. The only thing left for them to do is to disown her like she's never existed, like she was never a part of their flesh.

What's this girl to do in order to erase the shame and dishonour she's brought on her father's house. If she's honourable, she would take her own life. Maybe the child would go with her, or maybe he would go to an orphanage.

If that girl has ever visited an orphanage she would know that when you're young it breaks your heart that kids with large, dark pleading eyes capture yours and never, ever let you go.

They follow you around the rooms, always trying to be the one to hold onto you for the longest. The girl would know that it makes you cry and think of your own days as a virtual orphan when they take your hand and say, "Take me, Aunty." And they would have tears in their eyes when they look up at you. Then other voices would join in and say, "No take *me*, Aunty," even though they're only a couple of years younger than you.

Navin's mother wasn't particularly honourable – or maybe in fact, she was! She got together with a drunk. Perhaps at the time he was doing her a favour by taking in her and her baby as well.

***

After he'd signed the X on the dotted line and had received his wages, Navin's step-dad had gone straight to the rum shop as usual.

He came home later that night nearly unconscious. The baby was crying non-stop, and if his mother couldn't get him to shut up, Navin's step-dad knew just how. He picked him up by one leg and threw him out the window. Navin has been brain-damaged and epileptic since.

Navin, because he loves his parents and his siblings so much, does 'running-around' for people in the street to earn a little money, while some of his little brothers and sisters are at school.

When he's not 'working,' he's limping to and from the shops. He's one of the chief bread-winners of the home because he's the one who does the begging in the streets when the cane-cutting season is over and his step-dad wants a drink.

And because he's the one who comes to Miss Hyacinth for one thing or the other, several times a day, we became friends.

Navin came in tonight just after Miss Hyacinth had gone to bed, crying loudly as he entered to yard.

Before I looked out the open door to the complete blackness outside, I recognised his shrill voice, which escaped his lips with the saliva he couldn't control.

I also knew the lonely voice that came from his heart because it called out to mine.

I put down my books when I saw him limp in.

"What's wrong, Navin?"

"Me step-father beat me, Aunty."

"Why?" I asked, but I already knew they didn't have to have a reason.

"He drunk, and me mammy didn't want to give him me beg-money to buy ciggies."

Navin quieted down a little and limped upstairs to Miss Hyacinth.

"Miss Hyacinth! Miss Hyacinth!" he hollered. There was no answer.

"Miss Hyacinth! Miss Hyacinth! 'Is Navin. Ah come for cigarettes," but there was still no answer.

Through the thin floorboards of our ceiling, I heard her mumbling upstairs. I picked up my books again and worked by the light of the lamp on the floor.

I felt a grumble in my tummy and willed it to go away. I had kept some stale roti from yesterday, but that was for tomorrow's breakfast.

"Miss Hyacinth, 'is Navin, mon. Ah come for cigarettes. Ah really got to get them!"

After a few minutes of pleading, Navin walked downstairs, his uneven footsteps sounding like a lonely steelpan bass rhythm through the thin wooden walls.

I got up again and let my eyes follow Navin out of the yard. In the darkness, I could only make out the shine of his naked back against the dull moonlight.

It was time to shut the stable door. Apart from the millions of stars in the sky and the clouded moon overhead, there were no other lights. Everyone was indoors, probably asleep.

It would be hot with the door shut, but I still had to hide the fact that I was on my own.

Five minutes later, I heard a batter of drunken shouts from outside the door. My heart skipped several beats because I was still sitting right behind it.

Almost instantly, I recognised the voice to be that of Navin's step-dad. Clearly, he had stumbled near our door in his rum-induced fit.

Eventually, he found his way upstairs in the dark and banged on the old lady's door.

"Yuh betta get out here now, Miss Hyacinth. Ah ain't joking!"

He followed that up with something I couldn't make out.

Miss Hyacinth didn't mumble that time. She got up, dragging one foot behind her. I heard nothing for a moment then George's voice pealed through the night. He sounded even more intoxicated than Navin's step-dad.

"Ah will come out there wid me hammer and hammer yuh skull in! Say . . . say one more word and yuh blood will paint de steps in red!"

Drunk on drunk, Navin's step-dad knew who was boss. I heard him stagger downstairs and from behind the safety of my wooden door, I knew that Navin was in for a difficult night.

A Guyanese Proverb: Spit at de ski, it su fall ah yuh face.

Translation: If you spit at the sky it will fall on your face.

Meaning: If you resent others above you, it will only be to your detriment.

CHAPTER 7 – THE STREET

The street lacked a lot of things, but one of the ever-present elements was drama. Family drama spilled over and rolled into to Leroy's kitchen, where groups of strange men hung out in the evenings.

There was only ever a tiny handful of burglary in our street. But if you considered that most of the towns' burglars lived there, I suppose that's not surprising. No one burgles in their own backyard, especially since everyone knew everyone else so well.

The tiny amount of burglaries in our street was never solved because one calls the police. Most of the street people didn't *want* to call attention to themselves.

I heard more shouting than usual one evening. The normal hollering was interspersed with panicked screams, sure signs of street-wide activity. When I rushed out a fight was already in progress in the middle of the street, involving about twenty people.

The entire street was out for the evening's entertainment. They were either just arriving, or already standing around.

I asked someone what was happening and found out that a man who lived a few doors down from the yards had broken into his ex-wife's home. He broke in to get his work clothes from the wardrobe, because she wouldn't let him have anything from the house.

She screamed through her front window, 'Help! Allyuh, Help! Thief man! Thief man!'

That was all they needed – the men nearby came running to her rescue. They dragged the man into the street by his collar, and soon a group of them jumped into a pile, using him as a punching bag.

"Yuh don't burgle people in this street!" they shouted, to the man whose rum they once consumed. Within a minute, the fight-pot had doubled. Some people were even fighting each other! The action wasn't far from Leroy's house, so he pranced in – one hand on his hip, the other, holding his cheese grater.

He stood well outside the crowd, leaned over as far as possible, with his butt – clad in his cut-off jeans – sticking out in the air. He began to beat any part of *any* body he could lay his grater on. It seemed like he'd waited a long time to cheese-grater someone – anyone.

Shouting, screaming, laughing and beating at the same time, Leroy looked for bare backs, legs and arms and cheese-gratered them generously.

When emotions got the better of him and the dust of the fight kicked up a bit, Leroy stopped beating for a few minutes and jumped around on his toes, apparently looking for fresh skin he didn't think had tasted his grater. He then resumed normal cheese grater service.

I watched Leroy's dance. It was stunning! All the elements which made up Leroy shouldn't be put together to create a normal human being. For such a big, tall man with a gravelly voice, he had a very pronounced lisp, made worse by teeth which never quite found a home in his mouth, *and* a couple of other speech impediments.

His movements were extremely poised. Leroy had a way of bending over, as though he was stretching before a ballet lesson.

During the fight, his empty hand was bent at the elbow, palm facing out. He puffed his chest out, and a split second later, stuck his bum out. His hands then made half a circle, the empty one went to his knee then his grater hand did its thing with slow, elaborate flicks of the wrist.

Jerry Saunders, the bike man from Leroy's upstairs flat was standing next to me before I knew he was there.

"Can yuh believe this?"

"Why are they so angry with him?" I asked.

"It's *their* territory. It's like an insult for someone else to barge back in," Jerry Saunders said. I thought for the first time that he could be all right if he didn't try to talk me up every time he saw me.

"This is a perfect end to a perfect day," Jerry Saunders smiled.

"Yeah?"

Leroy was grater-whipping someone whose legs were the only part of his body I could see.

"Today is my son's birthday. Just spoke to him on the phone."

"Didn't realise yuh had kids."

"Yeah, just one son. He lives in New York with his Mum."

"Let me outta here!" someone screamed from the pile of bodies.

"I got a picture here," Jerry Saunders said, fishing into his back pocket for his wallet. He

clothing and pretend we were just clearing up or something.

We had three rules for washing in the morning; listen out for Miss Hyacinth at all times. Squat so that she couldn't hear the water falling on the ground (because you're taller when you stand up). Always take an extra piece of clothing in case she was too near for you to do anything else when you heard her coming.

When I opened the door Shanta, one the children who lived on the far end of our street, had a message for me.

"Yuh muddah say to come and meet she at our house."

"What?" I was confused. What was my mother doing at their house? Why didn't she just come home?

"Yeah, yuh muddah say to come. She at we house."

When I got over there my mum was standing under the front part of the house where the family dwelled. The kitchen in the back had long since fallen down.

I was expecting her to have lots of luggage, just like she did in the past when she returned from a foreign country. Instead, she had only two bags, one on her shoulder and a little one sitting on the ground between her feet.

She looked drained. The first thing she said to me was, "They tek all me things at customs."

I looked down at her feet because I didn't know how to react. We had survived largely because we thought our sacrifices were going to be fruitful. We thought we were going to have all we needed when our mum came back – and *then* we could live happily ever after with her.

If you're unlucky to come across an unsympathetic customs officer on your way into Guyana from Suriname, he could decide to take all of what you had – or just the things he fancied.

Sometimes traders bringing banned items like wheat flour and cooking oil made it through with their stuff by paying the customs officers 'a little something.'

Mum obviously didn't have that extra something, and it was clear she didn't want to share anything else with me.

I didn't ask for any more details and never got any.

But at last she was home! Whatever it was, we could suffer through it together. I could drop my shoulders and relax finally! I didn't have to pretend anymore. I took the bag she had laid between her feet and we began our short walk home. My mind was racing – going much faster than my feet.

What would she say about our empty room? Why *really* did she send for me?

Maybe she was ashamed? I did understand. Well, I think I *would* have understood if she'd given me an explanation. But that's the same thing, isn't it.

I mean, if you'd understand if someone told you something, do they need to tell you that thing if you would've understood anyway?

I felt I should say something about our furniture before we got home. My anxiety felt like a worm inside my throat.

It reminded me of when I was a little girl, living in a house where my grandmother kept a nursery school.

Our next-door neighbour had a big, high house, which sat on the highest stilts I'd ever seen. There was a large tamarind tree opposite their house and some people believed there was treasure buried under it. In fact, one woman even sacrificed a little girl to get her hands on the treasure.

I was standing on our veranda on a rare occasion one day, when I was about three or four. The kids from the high house were playing under their house. They were digging up the dirt, playing with water and getting mighty dirty. Suddenly, the littlest one screamed jarringly and pointed to his naked bottom. There was a long, brown shoelace hanging out of his body.

I ran to find my aunt Theresa, and she took me by the hand as we ran over to get a better look.

By this time, his mother had raced down from their high house. She washed his bottom while we all gazed at the stuck shoelace.

Once it was clean we realised that the hanger-on wasn't brown, but white. It wasn't 'hanging' either. It was *wriggling*.

The boy's mother told him to bend over but he wouldn't keep still. From the back, it seemed like he was imitating the wriggling thing, which was trying to escape him.

She finally grabbed hold of her son but couldn't make him bend over for her to get a better look, so she got one of her oldest boys, Rowland to hold his brother still.

With the little boy in a bent-over position, his mother pulled at the wriggly thing while the rest of us gaped on. After about the third try she pulled a worm out of the little boy's bottom and we scrambled in different directions, each with a different degree of disgust on our faces.

At the entrance to our yard, I told my mother about the furniture and the bailiff. She nodded. I think she expected it. Did they contact her *before* she left?

A Guyanese Proverb: Lil bwoy nah climb laddah to tun big man.

Translation: A little boy does not climb a ladder to become a grown man. (Or, climbing a ladder does not make a little boy a grown man.)

Meaning: You can't expect to be where you want to be without first spending time grafting, and gaining the experience it takes to get there.

CHAPTER 9 – SCHOOL FRIENDS AND ROB

As usual, I woke up early enough to catch Mass before going to school. After I got ready and walked the ten minutes to church, only a handful of people were there as expected – the older people attending, and the altar boys timetabled to serve.

I usually met with Sita, my friend of five years, in school these days because we now lived quite a long way from each other.

With Bibi gone, we picked up with Moira, who was also repeating the last year with us. Sita was back at school because her grades weren't quite what she and her parents expected. She knew she could do better. Me, I was in for the free ride.

I was trying some new subjects, but having only one year to complete a two-year syllabus, my chances didn't look too bright.

"I got some trouble with my parents," Moira told Sita and me when I got into school. Her swollen face was finally back to normal after the bee attack on our bike ride.

"What happened?" I asked.

"They found out about Rob, and they'll kill me when I get home this afternoon," she replied.

Moira had been seeing Rob, a married detective, for the last few months.

"Ah got to get out of school. Gotta see him to let him know that they know," Moira continued, wringing her hands.

"Can *we* come? We got a free period after lunch," Sita said.

"No," Moira answered, wiping her eyes. "But come home with me this afternoon so my parents wouldn't do anything rash."

She'd never wanted us to know about Rob, but the burden of the secret had crushed her so low, she eventually buckled under and told us.

She had all that I wanted – a loving family, a beautiful home, and good looks. And even though I couldn't understand why she had to have Rob, when she could have *anyone*, I wasn't going to let her down.

"You girls, what yuh up to today?" Moira's mother asked with one eyebrow suspiciously raised. Maybe she knew why we were there.

We said nothing.

"I think you're the three musketeers. Trouble, trouble, trouble, in *equal* measures," Moira's mother continued, but she was smiling. We waited for what would come next but she seemed very controlled. I knew it from the way she held her back when she turned away. I used to *have* to be good at reading backs. When she walked off, we breathed a sigh of relief.

"Ever noticed how we're never equal," Sita said, "How we're the first, second and third in everything?"

"What d'ya mean?" Moira asked.

"Well, Anne's the tallest, I'm in the middle and you're short. Then you're the richest, I'm in the middle again and Anne's poor. Then I'm more attractive, you're in the middle and Anne's . . ." Sita said.

"I'm still here," I replied before she could finish, feeling slapped in the face, but trying to smile through it while swallowing it down.

"Can't believe yuh just said that out loud, Sita," Moira said, shaking her head.

"No, but it's true," Sita said, turning to me, eager to get her thoughts aired without interruption. "Even our hair length; Moira's is the longest, mine in the middle and yours – the shortest. And . . . and look at me." Sita was ignited by the flow now. "I'm the fairest, Moira's in the middle and you're the darkest."

"But it's easy for *anyone* to be darker than you, Sita. And I don't see that much difference between us anyway," Moira laughed.

"Look, I'm going to change out of this uniform and go out with y'all."

Moira went into her bedroom and came out wearing some very tight jeans. I felt a pang of jealousy, as I've always wanted some.

We said goodbye to Moira's parents and left. When we got to the top of Moira's street, Rob was waiting for us. As I walked off home, I heard him say he was waiting for his guys because they were going on a job.

***

Please Prophet tell me what you see?

It has been snowing all morning. Gabriel my five-year-old son looks up to me and says, "Mummy, I'm cold."

"Come here, son," I say, pulling him close. We're standing in the playground waiting for the school bell to ring.

I hold him close to me, and we stand, him with his back pressed against my legs, watching his schoolmates running around and drawing silly pictures in the snow.

My hand is on his heart and I feel the thump-thump of it pumping warm blood through his little body.

I say a prayer of thanks to God. I say a prayer of thanks for this beautiful moment. I thank God for giving me life so that I could give this little being life – and love.

I say this prayer of thanks because even though I can remember a time when I was extremely sad, I can't recall what the sadness really feels like. It's been so long since I've felt that way.

I thank God for such a long absence of blanketing sadness, for Gabriel, for his beautiful, beautiful father; and for snow.

***

There was a mad rush with several voices shouting outside our house. Both Mum and I raced outside to look. We were just in time to see the tail end of a man trying to climb our front wall, which led to the side of Miss Hyacinth's property where her chickens were grazing.

He hesitated for just a second before changing his mind about scaling the clumps of barbed wire. With a deep animal sound in his throat, he suddenly made an about turn, jumped over the side fence, and ran into the nurse's (who lived at the front of Miss Bessy's yard) back garden.

He trod through the cabbage patch her young son so lovingly fostered, and scampered madly, hands in the air, into Miss Bessy's washing line.

As he did so, a policeman came running up, sweaty and puffy. He stood for a few seconds, hands on his knees, gulping down mouthfuls of warm air. He stared hopelessly at the runaway, as he revved out of sight. Swiftly following the cop, Moira's married boyfriend, Rob came running up, gun drawn.

"Yuh see him? Yuh see him?" he shouted.

I pointed in the direction he went. The policeman, not quite recovered, said to Rob, "He gone, boss man. He gone. I come in here and he just disappeared."

The policeman looked at us as if he was willing us not to speak.

"Just gone, boss man," he puffed again.

"We'll go round this way," Rob said and they jumped over the opposite fence leading to the squatting huts. I was sure the criminal was not going to be caught anytime soon.

CHAPTER 10 – T.N.M

It was nearing the end of my last year in high school. Mum said I should enrol in the typing school so there was some direction after my exams.

She found a job as a domestic at a local guesthouse and now we live like a proper family – a family I could be proud of. Nowadays I take every opportunity to bring into normal conversation, 'My mum *at our house* said this . . . My mum *at our house* said that . . .' I twist in the 'at our house' part because all my life I'd never been able to say anything as normal as that.

"We'll save up and get our things back," Mum said.

"That would be so nice. And then we can live a normal life again?" I asked her.

"Yeah. It hurts me that you guys have to go outside to talk to yuh friends; that you can't invite anyone home because there ain't no where to sit."

I shook my head and thought for a while. "Franc is home now, and Theresa's coming out of hospital soon. That's *much* better than it used to be."

I wanted to say that anything was better than being beaten and crushed like garlic, but Mum had been very quiet recently and I suspected she didn't want to be reminded of what we'd left behind.

"Maybe when we get our things back you can start to relax and not look so worn," Mum said. "Yuh putting far too much pressure on yuhself."

"Uh, huh."

"Maybe you could cut down them *Legion of Mary* meetings during exam time. Maybe you could do them once a week instead."

"Yeah, but if I don't go to the meetings I won't get allocated any weekly visits. Them old people at the home and the kids at the orphanage look out for me," I answered. "I can't let them down."

"As long's yuh sure," Mum replied. Then she went into her quiet world. She used this phrase to me often – to me, but to no one else. This phrase somehow made me feel like she was getting weaker. This meant I *had* to get stronger. The more she became the daughter, the faster I had to take her place. And if I had to be mother and protector to her and my sister, I'd have to learn pretty fast.

I was already an adult, but I felt I had to put up the front of creeping into their world inch by inch, just the way they expected me to. I would do my crawling in front of their adult faces without them seeing me and before they knew it, I would've arrived.

I spent Saturday mornings after Mass with Aaran's grandmother and another woman, making plastic and paper flowers. I watched their trained hands and imitated them precisely. I made sure they couldn't tell which flowers were their adult ones, and which were mine, and soon enough even *I* couldn't tell the difference. And before they knew it, I was the one wiping the statues and cleaning the brass and silverware for Mass instead of TNM.

Yes, I would invade their world without them seeing me; I had long since forgotten if I wanted to or *had* to. August was over, and in the space of a month, my childhood had flashed by.

I didn't mind taking TNM's place, I just didn't want to *be* her, especially since I was already so much *like* her.

TNM lived a few doors from the church. She never missed a *'Trust No Man'* preaching opportunity whenever she saw us girls standing near the altar boys, or playing table tennis with them. Even if she was merely passing by on her way back from the shops, she stopped by, pulled us aside, pointed a stubby finger in our faces, and repeated, *'TNM! TNM'!*

When she felt we were tired of that sermon, she crept up behind us whispered *'M.A.D'* in our ears. When we recoiled and looked back at her puzzled, she would nod her head as if she totally understood why we agreed with her – deliberately misunderstanding our disgust for approval.

None of us knew her name – or if we did we'd long since erased it from our memories. In her early fifties, TNM still lived with her mother. This was no surprise because if *'Men Are Dogs'* and 'couldn't be trusted', who would want to live with them.

TNM had one hair style; a part straight down the middle and two plaits joined at the back with hair pins. At church, she sat at the front with the rich, Portuguese parishioners, even though – like me – she's only part Portuguese.

She was a large part of the reason I changed my mind about becoming a nun. When I looked at her, I sometimes saw myself. Her life seemed to describe the core of misery, and that wretchedness seemed mainly because she wasn't loved.

Would I be as miserable if I got to her age and found that I was past having a husband and children? That I had no love?

Little did I know, I would have to digest my disgust of her. I would see the inside mechanism behind the ticking of her life, after she jumped to my rescue.

A Guyanese proverb: If dutty deh ah roof top, yuh barrel ah catch am.

Translation: If there is dirt on your roof, your barrel (a receptacle for catching rainwater in a country where the water system is not reliable) will catch it.

Meaning: children will behave the way they've seen their parents behave. (Or, on a personal note, kids will also learn to behave by seeing an example of what they don't *want to become).*

CHAPTER 11 – DAVE AND BRIAN

Dave had a houseful of sisters and I quickly became another one of them. Aaran had had her eyes on him for a very long time, but neither of them budged from their locked position. Dave and Brian were two of the constant altar boys I saw at weekday morning Masses.

Brian seemed to be the only person who didn't notice my old, faded clothes or that I never brought any tennis bats or new balls.

Brian never gave me any indication he noticed our opposites. While teaching me to cycle, he encouraged me to ride his new bike with just as much enthusiasm as I did his old one. And when I dented them, which was often, he brought another – sometimes his brother's – the following day. His new jeans were as good for wiping my blood (from my bruises) on as his old ones were.

At fifteen and learning to play table tennis, I found myself surrounded by bikes – many of the kids who played with me rode to Father's house. This was my first opportunity to closely inspect a bicycle and even sit on the seat.

Obviously, most of the kids didn't want me to learn to cycle on their bikes on a regular basis. Some were even embarrassed for me because I was pretty tall, and I was weaving and toppling onto the road in public view.

Brian – and sometimes Dave – held the seat steady as I jumped on. They ran up and down the street with me, past TNM's house. When I shouted 'Now' they let go. I'd peddle for a bit, then capsize. I was somehow never able to jump off before the bike hit the ground. This went on for weeks, but I persisted and so did Brian. He tried different combinations; extend handlebars, lower the seat, extend both, lower both, nothing worked.

"Look," Brian said one day. "Let me ride along with yuh. I'll keep holding the back of yuh seat so yuh could ride to the end of the street. "

"Yuh sure about that?" I asked.

"Yeah. I normally ride with one hand on the handlebar anyway. If yuh can ride for the length of the street it'll build your confidence better."

"I'm all over the road? Ain't I?"

"Uh, huh," he answered, with a smile on his face, "It's like yuh painting an imaginary zig zag line – but only four at a time, then crash!"

"Don't be mean! I left some of my skin on that road, yuh know!"

"Yuh know, ah joking! I'll take Dave's bike and you take mine."

It took me three or four seconds of erratic steering and zig-zagging on the road to crash into Brian with a mighty clang. We piled up into each other on the sweltering asphalt in the mid-afternoon sun in front of TNM's house.

Body parts mangled with metal and paint. I tried to get up, but found that my foot was attached to Brian's bike in some bizarre relationship.

"Don't pull!" Brian said. "Stay still for a bit."

"What, what's wrong with my foot?"

Brian finally got Dave's bike from under the pile. I noticed that the front wheel was pretzel-shaped.

"Hold onto yuh knee and keep your leg still," instructed Brian. I wondered why he was behaving strangely when all we did was crash into the road. I'd done that probably every day since I first jumped on a bicycle – and worse than this. Was he upset that I'd damaged the bikes? Had I damaged them beyond repair?

"I have to pull yuh foot out of the wheel. Ah think something's wrong here." Brian bent over and his hair fell over his eyes. Blood rushed to his face and made his pale skin almost bright red.

"Did you hurt yourself?" I asked.

"Dunno yet."

I brought my eyes round to where my foot and Brian's bike had married. My heel seemed welded to the spoke and wheel hub. The sight reminded me of the throwing-stars I'd seen in Chinese movies with my uncle Christopher when I was younger. In the blink of an eye, the Kung Fu Masters could flick the stars from their expert hands to deep inside the flesh of their enemies.

There was no blood – no pain. Brian looked at me and I looked at him.

"Yuh got hold of your knee?"

"Uh, huh."

"Pull?"

"Pull."

Blood squirted out onto the asphalt and sprayed the bikes. Before I knew it, Brian had his hand under my arm and was half-lifting me up TNM's stairs.

"Sit there," she instructed, pointing to a chair in the corner of her dark front room after she had let us in. Her mother sat on a dusty couch on the other side of the room, leg encased in clean bandages.

I looked at the dozens of small figurines covering each spare surface of TNM's living room. Holy Marys, little Jesuses, and what I could only guess were *Unknown Saints* peppered the room.

Most of them were dressed in dust. On the wall, there was a picture of someone who looked like a young TNM in a nurse's uniform.

When TNM appeared again, she was carrying a basin of warm water and a collection of cotton wool. I trusted her strong and confident hands as she took my leg between them. I felt sure she knew what she was doing. She didn't falter, nor did she hurt me once.

"Don't look now," she said when she'd cleaned most of the blood away.

This got my attention away from the eerie eyes-filled figures and the dusty frames of family pictures tacked to the wall. I looked down in time to see her stuff a piece of cotton wool, soaked in something yellow, in a hole in my Achilles tendon. When she drew back the flesh to do so, I saw a flash of white – cartilage maybe.

Brian may have seen it too, because a sharp, audible intake of breath escaped him.

"I'll put some dressing and a bandage on it, but yuh should go to hospital, or you might never be able to walk again," TNM told me.

"Yes," I answered, but I had no intention of going anywhere but back on a bike – though, in the other direction where she couldn't see me. I'd heard too many of TNM's dramatic, short sermons before. *But I thought she may have had a point when I was hobbling around for the next few weeks.*

"What's wrong with you? Don't tell the child things like that," TNM's mother said to her as she passed her couch to go back to the kitchen. TNM gave her mother a look sourer than the one she gave to us girls when she thought we're too close to the altar boys.

I waited for her to respond, maybe to address her daughter by name, but she resigned herself to looking at Brian and me across the room, adding yet another pair of empty, staring eyes on the fresh meat in the house.

I didn't know where to look, and maybe Brian was suffering from the same affliction because he said, "Um, we got to be going now," as he extended his hand to me.

"Mek sure she gets to hospital," TNM said to him, already back in the room.

"Okay," Brian answered.

"Thanks for looking after me," I said. Both Brian and I managed to speak to TNM without calling her by name.

"What's wrong with TNM's mother?" I whispered as we walked down the stairs.

"Dunno. She has a wheel-chair, I think."

"So she never goes out?"

"Don't think so," Brian answered. TNM's always rushing back home after Mass and meetings, ain't she? Maybe her mum can't move around too much.

"Reckon that's why she's so bitter?" By now we were outside the gate. Brian, at some point, while I was captivated by miniature, staring statues, had come downstairs and moved the bikes off the road and into TNM's front yard.

"Reckon she's angry she had to give up her life to take care of her mum?" I continued.

"Well, if she hates men so much, maybe she *did* leave home at one point. Maybe she had a problem with men and had to go back. She couldn't hate men so much unless she had a reason."

"Unless . . . unless it's her father she learned the hatred from," I said.

"Suppose. So, we going to hospital?"

"Nah."

"Okay, but you should lay off the bikes for today, not that you *can* ride mine anyway."

"Sorry about your bike, Brian."

"You reckon TNM used to be a nurse?" Brian said thoughtfully.

"Hmmm, she did seem to have a whole lot of cotton wool, didn't she? And her mum's leg looked like it was bandaged by a pro."

"I'll take you back to Father's house, then come back for the bikes, right?"

"Thanks, Brian, but I can push one."

"Sure?"

"Yeah, mon!"

"Okay. Let's go! Race?"

"Ha!"

I was laughing, but I was thinking of TNM and how deeply etched in sadness her face always was. I remembered her singing with gusto when I was a little girl, in the days when my then young Uncle Christopher was an altar boy.

Christopher loved Bob Marley and played him constantly when he came to visit. Nowadays, instead of in the army, he was wasting time in a prison in Suriname, where he had gone to find his fortune. I guess he was convinced there was a lot of money in illegal drugs.

My grandmother – Christopher's mother – was very proud of him and his altar position.

"Yuh the only black altar boy, there," she used to say with pride.

And when he took the wafers from the vestry and brought them home, she'd say, "Yuh will bring disgrace to me if they find yuh out!"

"I not the only one who take them!" he used to point out. "All them other altar boys tek some."

Then he would hand me some and I would eat them and wonder what they put in them to make them melt like a halo on my tongue.

The next time I saw Dave and Brian, Dave said to me, "The road workers called."

"What road workers?" I asked. I hadn't seen any 'road workers' in New Amsterdam for as far as I could remember. The pot holes had turned into man holes over the years and the drivers had long ago given up dodging them.

"Road workers," he repeated. "They said they received the sample yuh left them and the package with the replacement is in the mail."

"What on earth?"

Brian was giggling behind his hands, so much so I thought he was hiccoughing.

"*You* know, the sample you left for them to copy," Dave answered.

"She didn't get it, Dave," Brian was able to say finally, through his hiccoughing laughter.

"*What* didn't I get?"

"You just spoiled my joke, Anne. You know how long it took me to make that one up!" Dave shouted.

"He's talking about your bruises and the skin you left on the road," Brian said at last.

I laughed despite myself. "Not one of your best, but that's a good one, Dave."

"Why yuh tease her so much, eh Dave?" Brian asked.

"It's okay," I answered. "It's the price ah pay for being adopted as his younger sister."

"Younger sister?" Brian laughed. He's two years younger than *you*!"

"Long story, Brian," Dave said, running his hands through his huge afro. He was the only person I knew, who could maintain an afro with almost straight hair.

CHAPTER 12 – MY DAD

"I got to talk to you, Anne," Mum said when I walked into our house after school. She was cooking dinner on the one-burner kerosene stove so Franc could get some warm food when she came home. At six, she was finally able to live like a little girl should.

I wasn't going out much because of final exams. Margaret Lawrence and Razor Da Silva, radio announcers, were my constant companions while I studied. Razor had the best music programme on the radio. We didn't have the charts in Guyana like they did overseas, but if you wanted to know what was hot anywhere in the English speaking world, you had to listen to his show. He brought chart-toppers to his listeners, way before they were played anywhere else. And since we only had two radio channels, both owned by the Government, good music was hard to come by.

"Yuh father came to see me at work today," Mum said.

My heart sank because I'd done something terrible. My father had been visiting my mother at her workplace. He'd freshly broken up with his latest lady friend.

"Yuh know that letter you gave me to hand to him?"

"Uh, huh," I answered.

"Well he came back yesterday with the letter, all upset," Mum said. She went over to where her handbag was hanging from a hook on the wall and took out the seven yellow, lined pages I'd written. There were red circles in places, and other areas were underlined.

"Ah wanted him to know how upset I was with him deserting me and stuff. Ah wanted him to feel the anger I feel about him, Mum."

"Yuh father was really upset by yuh words, young lady," Mum said, holding out the pages to me.

"Mum, inside, I'm not the person *she* made me. I'm louder and clearer in here," I pointed to my chest.

"Sometimes I have to let *me* out. You know ah won't be rude. That's not me. But I gotta have some answers . . ." I was about to continue when I noticed Mum's eyes crinkling up at the corners. Was she crying? I never wanted to make want her cry.

"He circled . . ." she began, but couldn't continue. Mum broke down laughing, her eyes completely closed by this time.

"He circled all the things yuh said . . . that hurt him." Mum was now laughing uncontrollably, tears streaming down her face. She held up her fore and middle fingers and made three-dimensional quotation marks in the air when she said '*hurt him.*'

Finally, she gave me the letter so I could see for myself.

"This is good stuff," I said, after I'd re-read some of my writing. "Can't remember writing all this. You angry with me?"

"What? No! Yuh got a right to be upset with him, whether he thinks so or not. Respect and love don't come automatically, and he ain't earned them. Neither did I."

"But I give them to you, don't I?" I pleaded.

"Yes, yuh do."

"I thought yuh would be angry when you found out."

"Nah," Mum said. "Ah glad you write it. Is good to get all them things off yuh chest."

I didn't tell Mum, but I had a *lot* more on my chest to get rid of. Maybe now that I knew I wouldn't get into trouble, I could write him another letter – more heart-felt this time.

"He said he coming back tomorrow to give me a letter for *you*." Mum said wiping her eyes.

And this is how my father came to be a part of my life – for the first time in my life. Bad letters led to not-so-bad ones, to friendly ones.

***

Theresa was discharged from hospital but only stayed with us for a week. The four of us squeezed into our room and we managed to get a little fold-out bed from a friend for her to sleep on.

"Ah need me freedom," Theresa said. My heart felt full for her, as I imagined she would soar above the world, catching the fallen stars, thrown down especially to her. I wanted her to rip off the bandages she's been wearing all her life – bandages I know I was a big layer of.

"Ah going to live with this family and work with them," she continued.

"Yuh know them good?" Mum asked. "They will treat you good?"

"Yes, ah know them real good. Miss Hyacinth used to iron for them, and they nice people."

I wanted to tell her that it was time that she had a life apart from all our problems – and us, but I just hugged her and tried not to cry.

The same day she moved out, before I could begin to miss Theresa again, I had an unexpected surprise. While Mum was doing her twelve hours at work, Aaran came rushing in the door, breathless.

"Girl, ah got something exciting to tell you!"

"What's it? It's Dave, right?"

"No, it's not Dave. Before I tell yuh, you have to promise the answer will be yes."

"Yeah, yeah. What's it?"

"You promise?"

"Yeah, I promise. Just tell me!"

"Guess what? Ah been saving up for the last month and I got this!" Aaran exclaimed, thrusting a wad of money into my hands, "It's to get your stuff back from that nasty bailiff guy."

"How? Why?" I'd never *seen* so much money, let alone have it in my hands.

"I was really upset by everything and how it happened and everything," Aaran said. "Ah really can't get the image of them emptying the house out of me head, yuh know. Anyway, since yuh already said *yes*, your Mum can go and get it all back. And . . . and . . . I'm taking yuh out for a Chinese!"

"Aaran, where did you get all . . .?"

"No questions, Anne. Let's go out to eat. I want a nice, chicken fried rice. You?"

When you've lived your life not expecting people to care about you and love you, kindness like Aaran's made you feel guilty for accepting it.

Kindness felt wrong, like some sort of sin for which you had to say Glory-Bes and Hail Marys.

But after you've found a way to wade through the dense guilt, kindness makes you feel like you've put on red glasses. Everything seems warm, and red, and funny-looking. A red world makes you laugh, and once your warmth has boiled over, a red world makes your steam affect everyone you see. Your steam makes them look twice at you, wondering, but not knowing exactly what's different about you.

I wanted to put on red glasses permanently, so my world could always be red. I wanted to give everyone red glasses so they could see how steamy and warm and funny my red world was.

I was itching to ask Aaran how she'd managed to get that wad of money, but I didn't want to wash her kindness in mud. It was too red and glowy, and I wanted to keep it that way. I wasn't going to say Hail Marys for it – not even one!

Please Prophet, tell me what you see.

"Welcome to all our T.V viewers. Today we have a treat! We've invited some well-liked and respected women to join our discussions for National Women's Day . . ."

The T.V talk show host introduces the five well-dressed women he's invited on his panel. It's hoped that what they say on air would be meaningful but more importantly, that they would help change the lives of viewers – especially that of their young female fans watching.

The producer had said he wanted positive role models. But is it true that because one was famous, they were necessarily a good role model?

". . . And last but not least, former model, National Stage Actress and Radio Broadcaster Anne Lyken on our show today."

There's no clapping, no stage audience. That would cost too much for a new television company.

"Let's get started, shall we?" the host addresses his audience at home. One of them is particularly interested in the last guest:

"That's her! That's Anne! I have to call her again later to tell her I saw her on T.V. Why won't she speak to me anymore? I'll ask her who she thinks she is anyway? And why she's having my calls intercepted. She used to talk to me when I called her up to tell her how much I liked her shows. Now she screens her calls and tells me ah calling her too much. Wait, what's she saying?"

". . . We simply have to support our girls so they develop the confidence to speak out against things they are not comfortable with.

Sometimes women who end up feeling trampled are those who start out without the nerve to say, 'Hang on, I don't like this!' We're too afraid to barge our way out of uncomfortable situations.

We are not sufficiently confident to believe that what we think or feel is important enough to share with others, whether we share it forcefully or gracefully in our speech, firmly by our actions or even physically by active self-defence . . . ."

CHAPTER 13 – MY GRANDMOTHER

When Mum first told me that 'Mammy' my grandmother, was coming over for dinner, I was pretty nervous.

Would she come over and blowtorch my new life? Would she whip out her bullhorn and tell us we were doing *everything* wrong? Would she *Ha, Ha* in my face and say it was all a dream, and that I had to go back to her house and climb those treacherous stairs again?

I felt she would fuss that the stuff in the house didn't all have their front facing forward. The spoons hadn't faced up since we moved and the two chairs we had weren't at impossible angles. She would surely be whiplashed when she came into the house!

"Hello all," she said in her best teacher voice, as she waltzed in. Her flair was intact; her head was high, and her neck stiff – as usual. She looked every ounce as proud and as untouchable as she was.

"Hi," we replied.

"So yuh did good in yuh exams," she said before we had a chance to offer her a seat. She didn't say my name, but I knew she was talking to me.

"Yes," I replied.

"Me friend say she grand-daughter told her about how they parade yuh on stage and applaud yuh when yuh went back to school." My grandmother said this accusingly, as if the fact that I dared get some attention without her consent was wicked.

"Well, they didn't really *parade* us. They just called some of the top students on stage. They do it every year," I found myself excusing my *parading* actions. She had to know that it was nothing special at all, my mind said. I didn't end my sentence with a name. I didn't know what I was supposed to call her now.

"Yuh went to the graduation?" she said in the same tone, nodding in Mum's direction and taking a seat.

"Of course!" Mum answered, "Anne got a special academic achievement prize."

"So I do all the work and other people get the glory," my grandmother said.

"Wot you mean, that *you* responsible for she performing well and at the end of it all, I get to go to the graduation?"

Both Franc and I looked at them in anticipation. They remained silent, then my grandmother abruptly changed the subject and said, "Well, yuh hear about how Sister Mac want me to move out?"

"No. Why?" Mum asked.

"She say she wanna do repairs and give the house to one of she sons to live in . . . ."

After dinner, we walked my grandmother home. It had grown dark and all the little roadside stands were coming out.

The mini-business owners had their little flambeaus tied up against their stalls. Some were already doing brisk business – nothing like Leroy's, but of course, he'd already made his profits in the afternoon when many of them were still at work.

I was carrying a little glass jar my grandmother borrowed from us to get her medicine from the hospital the next day. She didn't have any at home, and if she turned up at the hospital without a bottle, she couldn't get her linctus.

Walking down the street with the bottle in hand reminded me of the trips I made to the shops to buy rum or soft drinks (or both).

You didn't get sold soft drinks unless you brought a bottle to replace the one you were taking away.

The night also brought back memories of going out in the dark, especially once when we had to go to the hospital at night, hoping that the shadows would hide the hole my grandmother made in my face.

As we neared my grandmother's house where I was once imprisoned, I saw a familiar face walking towards us.

It was Sandra Europe from my old Primary school, who called me 'Fire ant' because I was red. She threatened to beat me and my friends almost every day and made our lives miserable.

I didn't recognise her straightaway because she looked very different. For one thing, she was significantly bigger than she used to be. She looked at me, recognised me, started to smile but seemed to change her mind.

I waved at her anyway and didn't feel my heart leap. I didn't even look for my grandmother's approval before I did it. Something was changing in me. Or maybe I was just changing *into* me. The stars that blinked at me all those years ago were out. They had inspired me to reach for them. Tonight, they inspired me to do something else; fight for myself.

When Sandra Europe passed me, I noticed that she *wasn't* fat. She was pregnant. Funny that Sandra was never just Sandra. She was always Sandra Europe. Just like Jerry Sanders and all his pals. Idi Amin was never Mr. Amin or simply, Idi. I wondered why that was so.

Sandra Europe looked scared of *me,* when years ago, I was the frightened one. One day, my grandmother would – not be scared of me (I never want to bring fear to anyone), but would see my strength and recognise she failed to break me. That she had wasted years of back-breaking (for both of us) work, all for nothing.

On the way back home, there was drama at Leroy's house. Apparently, while cleaning up his kitchen, Leroy was attacked by one of his boyfriends. Leroy wasn't a dreary man, but this was the happiest I'd ever seen him. The beating made him proud to be the centre of attention – at last.

Apparently, Leroy, like every other day, had sold out his food. He usually kept a couple of plates stashed for his best customers. Today however, there was a mix-up with Teddy, the boy who worked for him. Thinking the food was meant for him, Teddy devoured it.

Between giggles, elaborate swings of his wrists, and loud, uncontrollable laughter, Leroy told us – and the crowd that gathered when he bawled for help – what happened.

"Well," Leroy began, with a hand on his hip, "He come by for he dinner, right."

Leroy raised his free hand with a flip of his wrist. He rolled his eyes in the direction of his kitchen, pushed his tongue at the top of his palate, and made a *'ta'* sound.

"Thtupid . . ." (his lisp, made it impossible to say 'stupid') "Thtupid Teddy ain't gone and eat all the man's dinner." (Leroy said 'ain't' when he meant 'did.'

Evening came and the man in question came round for some chomps. When he found that the dish *he* had been busy mouth-watering after all day had disappeared down *Teddy*'s gullet, he jumped on Leroy and pounded him.

"Tho, ah told him when he came . . ." here Leroy almost collapsed in a fit of laughter, and had to rest both hands on his bare, incredibly muscular knees to support his weight.

"I thaid," Leroy continued between giggles, "I thaid . . ." and at this point we had to wait to hear what Leroy was trying to say 'he said' to the man who beat him up.

"I thaid ith not my fault Teddy can't keep his skirt-wearing pig snout to himthelf,"

Mum, Franc and I left Leroy on his stage, explaining to the new people who'd arrived, why he was wearing a big bump on his forehead.

A Guyanese Proverb: Baby who ah cry a house and ah door ah same ting.

Translation: A baby who's crying at home (your child) and a baby who's crying at the door (a stranger's child) are the same thing.

Meaning: treat everyone (and everyone's children) the same way.

CHAPTER 14 – MY SIBLINGS

When my Dad told me he had a total of ten children (one adopted, one deceased), I almost swallowed my tongue. So it *was* true!

It filled my heart to know that I was one of so many, but I tried to block the niggling tentacles that came out behind my eyes when it got dark. He'd left me – a baby he had, in order to marry a pregnant woman so he could adopt *her* baby.

No matter how many times I repeated it, and in different ways, I boomeranged to the same questions. What was wrong with me? Was I not beautiful enough? Did I not look like he thought his children should look? Had I been too dark? Was the spring in my hair too coiled? Would I *ever* get over that?

My dad was now a regular visitor, and he arranged for Franc and me to meet my brothers and sisters.

We travelled into the tiny villages on a narrow, Bauxite-covered road, way past where the dollars had dried up and the county had forgotten to pave the road. After many years of absence, I finally got a look at my old Primary school when we passed that way. We passed farming communities and came to villages I'd never heard of, with strange names like *Sisters* and *Brothers*.

All of the kids were ready and waiting. The mothers were present, cooking up a storm for our visit. I looked at all the striking faces, some of them similar to mine. The introductions felt like an hour in my head, and I temporarily forgot the names flying around as soon as I'd heard them; all except for the tiny, beautiful last child's (whose picture I saw, but had to wait to meet). She had *my* name – both of them!

We were in the same boat – the two of us. We were caught in the twisted nets of dysfunctional adults posing as parents, who didn't think of how their actions affected their young. The tentacles rose inside me again and I imagined my father back-handedly putting me aside, pushing me way behind him, and taking up a new baby, giving her the name of the one he thought he'd finally gotten rid of.

I shook my head free of this image. I wanted to enjoy *all* my siblings, adopted or not. Like me, they knew nothing of the world our parents were cultivating for us to live in. Without knowing them individually, I loved them all instantly.

Franc and I had one ritual to take part of. It was the one I suspected each visitor had to, even before entering the home. By hand, we were taken to the backyard to see the pond in which Sandra, one of my sisters had died.

Sandra had toppled into the pond after being sent there by one of their step-mothers – a particularly nasty one. This angry, violent woman had sent her with a large bucket to fetch water for the kitchen.

I stood rooted to the spot for a long time, together with one of my newfound sisters, Sue.

"I can't swim either," I told her. In a flash I felt an uncanny bond to Sandra, my dead sister who I'd never been given the chance to meet. I felt like I'd already understood her and the burden of the wickedness she must have had to bear. When you're a weak sapling and a mother who's not *your* mother hates you, she won't let you get your head above the dirt. There's no way to escape her punishments for the crimes you commit for being you.

"What yuh say?" Sue asked. She seemed to have caught and joined my trance.

"I can't swim either . . . like Sandra."

"Who? Sandra? No, she could swim like a fish, mon."

"Why did she drown, then? In a small pond?"

"Is a deep pond. We think the big bucket dragged her down. Was too big for she."

"Couldn't she call for help?"

"Daddy thinks she *did* call for help, but that no one hear she," Sue answered.

"So sad," I said.

"Yeah. We not over it. Daddy really sad," Sue said, looking up to me. "You really tall, like Daddy. And you talk nice, not like country people."

"I get teased, but I do it anyway," I said. I looked at her to find some facial similarities between the two of us, but I could see none.

That afternoon, we played and ran around their large garden. I was curious to know which of the mothers bore my various siblings and Sue pointed them out for me.

Nine of us decided that it was a good idea to go to our house and camp out there for the night.

"Yuh don't know how small our place is," Franc said.

"Ner'mind," one of my brothers answered. "We accustomed to sleeping four and five in one bed. Yuh got to do it head to toe, mon."

"But we only have one bed and a fold-out cot," I told him. "We'll have to sleep on top of each other." Everyone laughed.

"Yes, let's do it!" Sue said. "It'll be fun."

We asked my father – who was 'Daddy' to everyone else (Franc and I didn't know what to call him) – to take us back to town.

"Ah have to go to work," he said, "But I can give yuh money to catch the bus into town."

"Daddy, can we go to the cinema too?" one of the younger ones asked.

"I ain't got money for all of yuh," he answered. "Yuh sure ya'll will fit at Aunty Esther's house tonight?"

I knew it would be a tight fit, and so did he, so I didn't bother to answer.

Our room was about seven miles from where we were, but once the crowd of us had waited about twenty minutes with no bus in sight, we had a change of plan. We would walk all the way, trying to use as many short-cuts as they knew. We would use the money we had to go to the cinema anyway.

In groups of twos, we trekked the Bauxite-covered main street. Each time a vehicle went by, we turned our backs to the road because of the red billows of dust the wheels scooped up.

"I got dust in me mouth!" Franc cried.

"Well, yuh lucky it's not raining today," Sue told her. "You should see the mucky slush ah get on me uniform when ah walking to school on rainy days."

"Yuh walk all the way to school from here? It must take you hours!" I said.

"Well, I used to walk every day when my step-mother lived with we. Once Daddy went to work, she never gave me any money to catch the bus."

"And what did he say?"

"Ah don't think he knew, Anne."

"Well, what did he say when yuh came home hours late after walking back?"

"Nothing."

"Did you meet any scary people on the road?"

"Sometimes," Sue laughed. "But the main thing is, I know a lot of short-cuts to get into town!"

Our oldest brother kept the pace, and since I was the only one with a watch, I kept time. It looked like we weren't going to make the film, but there were a few short-cuts still left to explore.

As our group passed my old Primary school, I could almost smell the dust in which we played our hopscotch – the twins and I.

"I once saw a dead body there," I pointed out to my siblings the spot in which I and my friends, Raf and Tas stood as the body floated by.

"No way!" one of my sisters said.

Like a group of ducks, we crossed the road to get a closer look. My old friends the four-eyed fish were busy eating, two eyes on us, two eyes on lunch, as usual.

My younger, shorter brothers and sisters were awed by my story. And it was only then that I realised I'd never spoken about it before. Did all the talking we did on our lengthy trip loosen my tongue? Or maybe I finally felt that I could slowly unplug my fountain of pent-up misery.

The movie we wanted to watch had already started by the time we stumbled into town, so we went straight home.

After dinner, some tackles and races round the genip tree, we were ready to settle down. It took Miss Hyacinth three sessions of shouting and a couple of mouthfuls of her best grumbling to get the kids to quiet down.

By now I'd learned all their names. Apart from me, my namesake sister and one other brother, my father had given them all names that started with his initials.

That night we just about managed to fit us all laid out on the floor, head to toe, squeezed against each other. We made a human carpet, stretching from one end of the tiny room, to the next.

It reminded me of the day I went to Navin's house and saw some rolled up rice bags under the dining table.

"What are those for?" I asked his mum. "You guys got a lot of them."

"Is where we sleep," she'd answered, stretching out her arm to swipe under the table. "The place very small, so them little pickney sleep on the floor, here under the table."

"Where does Navin sleep?"

"He sleep up here," she said, again pointing to the table."

"He sleeps on *top* of the table?" How does he get down?"

"He jump down in de morning," she answered. "We only gat one bed," she said when I laughed. "Only me, me old man, and the baby can fit in it."

Mum always said she didn't know what new ingredient my questions had in them that made people feel they *had* to give an answer.

What I didn't tell her was that the ingredient wasn't new. It had just never been mixed up before – beaten, but never mixed.

Not long after my siblings' visit, I was introduced for the first time to my uncle John. He only had a little time because he was catching the ferry back to Georgetown.

It was great that I'd managed to see him then, because in a short space of time he became ill and didn't quite recover entirely before he passed away.

I thought my father was tall, but this man was taller. His hair glittered in the sun and shone like gold as he walked towards me. If he were decades younger, he would be a twin of my friend, Brian.

He stood outside the stable door as we made our introductions and when he rushed away, that was the last I saw of him.

I felt cheated not knowing this man all my life; cheated for not being allowed to spend time with him, and cheated for not being able to have a good conversation with him.

CHAPTER 15 - SOLLY

The yard we lived in was owned by the family of the lady who lived in the front house. Elaine was about Sasha's age. She was getting ready to migrate to Canada, where her parents and five brothers already lived.

One of Elaine's brothers was returning briefly to Guyana marry his sweetheart.

"Is not one of them visa weddings," Sasha explained to me one afternoon.

"What? Like when people pay someone loads of money to come back and pretend-marry them?" I asked.

"Yeah. It's not like that. Ah don't think the girl's family could afford a visa wedding anyway."

"Is it expensive to have a visa wedding?" I asked. If you wanted to know something current, Sasha was the person to ask. She spent her time doing housework, looking after her baby and digesting ear to-the-ground information.

"Oh, yes!" Sasha exclaimed. We were slouching on her stairs, airing ourselves in the warm afternoon breeze. She was on the step above mine and I could see she was starting to age. She'd told me she *wasn't* twenty-nine, so I guessed she was early thirties. Her straight, silky hair was still *naturally* dark. Mum was doing her daytime shift and Franc was in the street, playing hopscotch with the other kids.

"But is worth it in the end," Sasha continued. "Yuh wait a few years then yuh get to go overseas!"

"Do you have to *stay* married?"

"Nah. Only until a certain amount of time pass and then yuh can get divorce papers."

"Then you'll be a divorcee without even enjoying a proper marriage? Doesn't sound like it's worth it."

"Yuh young. This place so hard. Is worth anything to get the visa. I told you about me friend, dint I?" Sasha lightly backhanded me on the arm.

"What? The one who divorced his real wife to come and marry her cousin?"

"Yeah. But he wife was the one who set it up. They got ten grand – Uncle Sam money – for that, yuh know!"

"So Elaine's brother's wedding is for real," I said, "They really love each other like a proper wedding."

"Yep. Solly said it's gonna be a massive do."

Solly was Elaine's oldest, and only remaining brother in Guyana. He looked after the family's cattle and often boasted that he was the only person in the entire county who still had Guernsey cows.

"Why don't you live in the family house, Solly?" I'd asked him once.

"Me and me wife don't want to bring the kids up in this street," he had said. "Ah worried sick for baby Ella growing up here."

"Why doesn't your brother come and take her to Canada, then? She wouldn't be here, living with Elaine, if he wasn't taking so long to get his wife and baby out to where he is."

"True, Annabella," Solly had said to me, shaking his massive neck. His frame had long since overthrown the two-hundred-pound mark, and being over six-foot tall, he was giant-sized.

"Yuh right about that," he'd continued. "But it's not for me to say. I don't know their problems. Not everyone can have a perfect marriage like mine and Lisa's."

He had burst out laughing at this point, but I knew he was serious. He didn't want me to think he was boasting, but I loved his romantic stories and secretly treasured his pride in his marriage.

"Speak of the devil!" Sasha said, and brought me out of my daydream.

"Can't stop talking about me, Sash?" Solly laughed. He took his handkerchief out of his back jeans' pocket and wiped the sweat running down from his shiny, bald head. The sun glistened on his damp, black forehead.

"Go ahead and talk. Lisa won't mind."

"Was just telling Anne about the wedding, Mr. Smooth!"

"Yeah, that's just what ah dropped in for, Annabella. Yuh wasn't around last time I popped by," Solly said, looking at me. "I want to invite you to my brother's wedding."

"Would love to come! But can I bring my Mum and sister too?"

"Course! The more the merrier." Solly leaned his frame against Uncle's bannister and the stairs moved slightly.

"Yuh gon bring down the whole house!" Sasha screamed, and Solly swiped his wet handkerchief in her direction.

"Where's the wedding gonna be?" she asked.

"G.T.U hall," he said.

I thought about the big affair when the Comrade Leader opened the hall. He sang *Bringing in the Sheaves* and made everyone give money in a basket, which he said it was for the building fund or something like that.

"We having a massive 'Quey Quey,'" Solly told us. "Ever been to a Quey Quey, Annabella?"

"No."

"Yuh know, Quey Queys started in Africa as pre-wedding celebrations . . ." but he didn't finish.

"Yeah. We know all about Quey Queys Solly," Sasha laughed. "Yuh don't have to give the history of everything."

"But ah like his histories of everything," I said. "He knows more about everything than anyone else."

Solly laughed his drilling laugh, which shook his entire body. Sasha went to fetch him a glass of water and the two of us talked about school. Solly's voice was as clear as the whistle of the blue-sakie's early morning song.

"Ah have a brother a little older than you," Solly said at last. "Still at University. He would love you."

"Yuh can't really know that. We've never met." I said, and I felt my face go red.

"Nah, don't be embarrassed. There is no reason why Des won't like you, right Sasha?" Solly asked, taking the glass of water from Sasha's hand.

"Oh yeah," Sasha agreed taking her seat again, "He would love Anne."

"You making a match or something?" I asked Solly.

"Well, ah tell yuh something," Solly began, with his hand on his heart. When Solly said this, it was a good idea to settle down for a lecture. "Ah love all me brothers. Yuh can't blame me for looking out for them. Ah always on the look-out, cos ah want them to have what I have. Me wife was never about what she could get. She was all about me, and how she could look after me. She's a decent girl, and thems hard to come by these days."

"Solly, Anne don't believe nice things about sheself. She's never been told nice things."

"Used to!" I cried. I wanted Sasha to know there was a 'used to' me. *She* was sometimes called *Ann*, not *Anne*, and certainly not Anna*bella*.

"It'd better be, 'used to,'" Sasha repeated.

"Lemme know who them people are that hurt you, Annabella, and I will grind them!" Solly said, crushing one large fist into the palm of his other hand, his clear voice almost in a whisper. "I explained to you why I call you, Anna *Bella*. From the first time I saw your beautiful face, I knew you were as pure as a soft prayer."

"Where yuh get these things from, Solly?" Sasha laughed. "Why you a farmer, I would never know. Yuh should be a philosopher or something."

"I'm a farmer, because I *choose* to be a farmer, Sash. I talk to my cows and they listen."

"Yeah, right."

"It's okay," Solly raised both his hands in the air. "It's okay not to believe me."

"*I* believe you," I said. "Ah talk to people who're not there and have conversations with myself. So what's wrong with talking to cows."

Nearly an hour later, Solly was telling us about King Henry VIII, when mum came home from work. Franc skipped in after her, burnt almost red from playing in the sun. But she had a little-girl's smile on her face and I liked that.

"Mum, can I go and help Solly take his cows home?" I asked. "Me and Sasha are also taking baby Jay on the Back Dam for a walk."

We took the Back Dam Road and walked towards Stanleytown. Solly walked through the town in the evening, gathering his cows as he went. They grazed wherever they wanted to – eyes stapled to the nice, green grass. They covered miles without once looking up to see where their dinner-lunch-brunch-breakfast had taken them.

Before long we spotted one of Solly's cows a few yards away. She was sitting in the middle of the road, worn out, soaking up the heat from the asphalt. Before we could get to her, the driver of a passing car step out of his cabin and gave her a sharp slap on the back. She sat, unconcerned, chewing her cud, tasting the fresh grass she'd covered miles to savour.

Solly calmly walked up to her and called her by name. She got up straight away and turned into the direction of home. Solly saluted the driver of the car and he saluted back.

As we walked on with our eyes peeled, looking for more spotted cows, Solly told us of the alligator who lived in the Back Dam trench. "He eats dogs and rats, and there's plenty round here."

"Don't listen to him, Anne! Alligators don't live round here," Sasha said.

"There was only *one*. The people in this area," Solly said, sweeping his hands in front of his massive body, "They never had to put out rat poison. The alligator was their trusted rat-catcher."

"Miss Hyacinth puts out lots of rat poison," I said. "She don't want the rats to eat her chickens, so she's always got little bowls of poison set out around the place."

"It's the smell that ah don't like," Sasha said. "There's nothin' stinker than a poisoned rat left to rot in its own juice."

"They crawl under our floorboards when they feel ill. Then they get stuck, swell up, and die," I told Solly.

"That's nasty! You ever get them out?"

"We sometimes get stuck with them for weeks – months. Yuh know our floorboards are on wooden beams which sit on the bare ground . . ."

". . . And they have to rip up the floorboards each time, just to find the rotting rat," Sasha continued.

"How d'ya know where on the floor to start ripping?" Solly asked.

"Ah crawl on the floor and sniff to see where the stench is strongest. Imagine living in a small room like that with one or two dead rats, swollen with poison, bursting and rotting right under your feet – not inches away – *right* under yuh feet."

"Literally, Solly. Literally. The dirt comes through the floor when there's a flood," Sasha confirmed.

"Y'all stop. Ah feel sick. Seriously?"

"Seriously," I answered. "So I go down on my hands and knees and sniff. When I think I've found the stinkiest spot, I get the hammer and rip the nails out of the floorboard."

"What happens if yuh can't find it?"

"Ah hammer the board back in, and dig out another one. Sometimes I can see the outline of a swollen body under there, lying in the dirt, just out of reach. Sometimes I take out the board which is right next to the beam and the dead rat is *just* beyond it."

"And are the rats, rotten, burst, what?" Solly asked.

"Well, it depends on how long they'd been there," I answered. "Sometimes they're just *about* to burst. Sometimes they're already rotten. And it's my job to take them out, coz no one else wants to."

"What? Yuh mother won't take them out?" Solly asked.

"No, they make her retch. If ah don't do it, they'll get left there and we'd have to smell them for a whole lot longer."

"I can smell the stench from my steps," Sasha said.

"It's embarrassing," I said. "If a friend stops by ah can't let them come in because the smell is so bad, it's *all* you can do. You can't think, speak, sleep, nothing. You just have to *smell* that smell."

"Arrrrh!" Solly said, shaking his head.

"The tail is the worst bit," I confessed. "Sometimes ah take off the wrong floorboard. And after the third try, I'm scared Miss Hyacinth will shout down that we're breaking up her house, so ah just have to steel myself to feel around until I touch something. The tail and the dirt are the same colour, so sometimes I can't really see it.

When I touch it, I just have to grab hold and pull slowly so ah don't break up the body. I hate rats' tails with a passion!" I said.

"Tails are not so bad," Solly said, changing the subject. "When that alligator stopped eating rats and started hunting dogs and cows, them young men jumped in the trench, killed him and made curry with his tail. He had a nice, fat one."

"Reminds me of the story about those men up the Berbice river," Sasha said.

"Which story?" Solly asked.

"Din't yuh hear the story of the men who caught and skinned a jaguar? Them brought the meat into town and sold it as cheap beef."

My rat story wasn't finished, and I wasn't going to allow them to change the subject without hearing me out.

"You guys know that cockroaches eat rat dung, right?" I didn't wait for them to answer because I felt Solly might have a lengthy story about cockroaches stored up his sleeve. "Well, the cockroaches feed on the dead rats, then they run up our walls like upside-down rain."

"Oh, Annabella . . ." Solly began.

"Yuh wouldn't believe how *many* roaches we have. They cover the walls. And I mean *cover* – like paint, when they're running up and down." I was finally done, so I let Solly tell us about the finer points of cockroaches.

CHAPTER 16 – SUE

My sister Sue came to live with us. She told me she saw someone once who resembled the image she'd *made up* of me. She ran after the girl and asked her what her name was, hoping it was *Anne*.

While *I* was too busy staying alive to think about them, Sue was dreaming of me (once she was told I existed). I discovered that she played a major part in my father making contact with us.

"Ya'll related to that Lyken girl from Catholic church?" her next-door neighbour's daughter had asked her, when she was about ten.

"Which girl?" Sue had asked.

It didn't take her long before she convinced her friend next door to take her to church so she could see the 'Lyken girl' she mentioned.

Then the nagging started. She begged Dad over and over to bring her to see me. Is that why he didn't tell the kids of my existence until he *had* to – until I was a teenager? Perhaps he knew that Sue, in her tenacity would bug him to seek me out? I have these questions, but no answers to them.

"It's so hard each time you go home," I said to her.

"Yeah. We got so much sistering to catch up on."

We were lost when we weren't together, and soon, the natural thing was for her to move in with us. Our house was nearer to her school than hers was, and my father trusted that my mother would take good care of her.

With Mum and Franc still asleep, Sue and I got up before the crickets had properly gone to bed and went for long runs together. When Mum did the night shift (and had to sleep over at the guesthouse), together Sue and I took up the slack and looked after Franc.

In the afternoon when Franc was out playing, we sat outside on the driftwood that Mum and I had found and nailed together to make a bench. It was bathed in silvery sunshine in the daytime, but in the evening before the crickets returned, it was canopied by the genip tree. Mum and I had also covered a large part of the dirt outside our stable door – at the front of the house – with old wood we'd gathered. We scrubbed the wood with little tin scrapers and created an outdoor floor to keep our room clean.

Sue and I sat close together and exchanged stories. We found out that at one point in our lives, we lived just a few streets away from each other. She and Franc attended the same Primary school for a while, perhaps bumping into each other, but not knowing their lives would be linked together soon.

"Yuh know," I said to her, "All my life I wondered if it would've been easier to live with my father – our father. (I still couldn't call him *Daddy* like she did). From what you've said to me, I'm not sure now."

"Well, I was the one – Sandra and me – who followed Daddy everywhere he went. The others didn't have such a hard time with step-mothers and all that."

"You blame him?"

"No. Daddy always tries his best. Yuh don't really know he."

"Ah know this is our sore point. You love him, so you'll find a way to excuse and defend him. I'm not ready to do that."

"Ah know. But as yuh said, this here . . ." Sue waved her hand between the two of us, "This is *our* relationship."

"We're not responsible for what happened before us or around us," I continued, "Or for what he did and didn't do."

"Exactly!" Sue answered. "Me and Sandra, at least we got to go to school. Some of the others had to live so far out of town cos they were so poor, they didn't get sent to school a lot."

"How can *anyone* bring kids into the world and let them suffer like we did?" I asked. "Now ah feel like he was glad he kicked me out of the picture and never talked about me, because ah was one less mouth to feed."

Just a few weeks before Sue came to live with us, my heart was broken once more. During the week-ends when Mum was doing her long hours at work, Aaran came over and spent the days with me. We'd cook, sing at the top of our voices, and fetch water from the front pipe.

She brought her cigarettes over because she got some peace at our place when Mum wasn't there. Miss Hyacinth cleaned the Opposition Party's office on Saturday mornings so we never expected her to be at home during that time.

One Saturday, she forgot her keys for the office and came back early. If Miss Hyacinth had walked in five minutes earlier, she would've seen Aaran sitting on her top step, with me on the second, while Aaran combed the nits out of my hair, singing at the top of her voice.

What Miss Hyacinth saw instead, was Aaran on her own, puffing away on a cigarette. What happened next happened very quickly, and without the use of a phone – as only the people at the top of the street had them.

At Mass on Sunday, Aaran gave me a look from a distance that told me one or both of us was in trouble.

I kept my distance, and the fact that she sat at the front with her mother, told me that whatever it was, was pretty bad.

"They know," she whispered to me, once we'd found a place to talk.

"Know what?"

"Miss Hyacinth told them about me smoking."

"What? What did she say?"

"That they should stop me from going to yours. Ah can't come to you no more, Anne. Ah banned from ever coming to yuh place again."

"But that won't stop you from smoking, That don't make sense."

"Ah sorry, Anne," Aaran's eyes glistened over. "But she said that you're bad example. That she saw me and you smokin' and shoutin' and stuff."

"And you didn't tell them the truth?"

"Well, ah couldn't. Ah was so scared of how they reacted. Ah really sorry."

"It's okay. I would've done the same thing," I told her.

"I'll see yuh some afternoons under Father's house?" Aaran asked.

"Yeah. I'll wait for you outside your street."

As I walked home, I tried to work out what else Miss Hyacinth could've said about me that was bad enough to merit the ban. I had a clear idea *why* she'd said that, but I wanted to know what more she'd made up.

Aaran's family were well-respected in town, and Miss Hyacinth had even done ironing for them in the past. She was from the old-school who thought that white-skinned people were better than the rest of us. On her scaffold, Aaran was swinging from the top, I was somewhere in the middle, and she was sucking the dew at the roots.

Therefore, Aaran could not have been doing anything bad without *at least* half my influence.

After that, Aaran was put on a very tight leash. Our meetings were snipped short, and even when we waited around for each other in the streets, we had to look around to see who was watching. I felt like someone had ripped my twin-sister off my side. But I told nobody because I didn't know anyone who liked raw wounds.

A Guyanese Proverb: Dag buy rum, cow ah drink am, hog in sty get drunk.

Translation: Dog buys rum, cow drinks it, hog gets drunk.

Meaning: We're all in this life together. Be careful what you do, because other people are affected by your actions.

CHAPTER 17 – A DIRTY MOUTH

"We going to see Theresa tomorrow," Mum said to Franc and me one evening.

"Really? They gonna finally let us see her?" I asked. "They don't really think we *believe* that she's never at home when we visit?"

"Maybe they think we're stupid. They keep she in the house to do nothing but work. Ah can't for the life of me, think why they won't let us see she."

"They probably think we'll tell her they're using her or something," I agreed. "We have a right to meet. She's family!"

"They know she can't hear the doorbell, so they take advantage of that. Ah thought they were good people."

"Not so good at all," I said. "Last time I stopped by there after school, the lady came out and scowled at me. She actually shushed me away with her hand. 'Theresa is not here. Now go on your way,' she said in her stupid, high squeaky voice."

"Ah don't know what to do and how to get to see her."

"I'll think of something, Mum. Don't worry."

Neither of us needn't have worried because the next morning something unexpected happened, which meant that we couldn't go after all.

It was pretty early on Saturday morning, before Miss Hyacinth had dragged her bad leg downstairs to feed her chickens. I thought I was dreaming about her. In my dream, she was fretting with someone about a child. Was the child hurt? Was it her child? The dream went on like a stuck record, and soon the person was no longer talking in hushed tones. She was shouting.

I realised that I wasn't dreaming when the person walked heavily up Miss Hyacinth's front stairs. We woke up in a daze, but before we could open the back door to see what was going on, Sue whispered in a panic, "It's my mum! It's my mum!"

I looked at Sue, and the terror she was wearing on her face was one I knew intimately.

We sat quietly in the house, and listened to her carry on, hoping she would get tired and slink away. She called on several gods to witness her plight of how the black woman had kidnapped her child.

"Me no want me child to live with no black people!" she said. Then she darkened the air with language so fowl, I thought she was speaking in a different language.

Miss Hyacinth plied her for information and she supplied. Some of what she was saying, I never even knew. It was clear she was here to shame my mother so she could get her daughter back, a daughter who came of her own accord.

"We can't stay inside, Mum." I said, "She won't stop. You gotta tell her something."

"Ah don't want to go out there," Mum answered. I had a feeling that little by little, ever since that day I rescued her with the bag between her feet, tiny things were becoming too much for Mum to handle. And this was monstrous!

"It's what she does," Sue finally said.

"Wait, she's done this before?" I asked.

"Yes. She follow me round wherever ah go, and make trouble so ah can't stay there no more. She got nothin' to give me, and would find it hard to send me to school. But it's what she does."

As if she heard us, the lady outside said, "Yuh want me to kill meself? Come out and face me and give me back me daughter, you thief!"

"Ah have to go," Sue said, "Ah have to pack up and go. She won't leave me alone."

"But I want you to stay," I said.

"I *want* to stay," Sue said. But she was dejected and I knew – even together, we couldn't fight for her.

"Ah gon bring the police on you, you black theif!" By now Sue's mother was screaming and had probably woken up our neighbours.

"Ah can't have this kind of thing going on in me place," Miss Hyacinth said. "Ah not accustomed to all this fighting and cussing."

Susan went out and told her mother that she needed a few minutes to pack her things.

And this is how the still-raw Aaran-sized rip in my side was slashed open again.

Miss Hyacinth threatened us later that if Sue's mother ever came back, we'd have to move. We knew we couldn't afford to go anywhere else.

Please Prophet, tell me what you see:
With the rest of her Sunday school class, she walks up to the platform on which our Minister stands to give his sermon. She pauses to look around to the sea of friendly faces behind her – each one smiling, willing the class to go on and do us proud. There are no front-seaters or special

members; no catechism to learn and no idols in the wings.

They are people she's known since she was a baby, ever since my husband and I moved countries for the third time. All of them are people she's eaten with many times. Many of them have fellowshipped at her home, or she in theirs. She's our third and last child and our pet name for her is Momo.

She's the tallest in the class by far – and the oldest too. Her Sunday School teacher said she's more like one of the teachers now. She helps the others learn and do their craft, but that's her nature. She's always been sweet.

I look at her expression as she settles in and see much of myself in her. Her face could be a sketch of mine, made from one of the four pictures I have of myself as a girl. I wonder who could bear to be unkind to such an angelic face. I wonder how untidy a mind would have to be for hands to reach out and punch a face like that.

It's the annual Mothers' Day presentation, and her class will tell us why they love their mums.

It's her turn and she takes a deep breath. 'Go Mo!' I say to myself.

"I love my mother because she's the best person I know. I wish everyone could have a mother like her. She thinks of everyone before herself and she makes everything better for other people. She's very wise and gives good advice to others. I will be happy if I grow up to be just like my Mum!'

In my seat I dry my tears, and when Maz, my friend sitting in front of me turns back and says, "That's so true." I cry some more.

I have prayed to God so many times for so many things, all of which He has given to my children, some of it, through me.

And it seems I didn't learn to 'mother' from example. What better blessing is there!

CHAPTER 18 – A LIFE-CHANGER

And then *change* attached itself to the third wheel of a clock and wound its hands around my life. It was just around the time when Mum started spending her free time standing at the door and casually staring out past the large genip tree.

As I was walking back home from morning Mass, I heard running footsteps behind me. I knew that when I turned around it wouldn't be someone I knew. Even though they didn't know why, my close friends knew the effect running footsteps had on me.

"Scuse, me! Scuse me!" the woman panted when I whirled around, "Didn't mean to scare you."

She was wearing an apron, which came half-way up her long legs, and was carrying a pair of scissors loosely in her hand.

Standing opposite me, she looked directly at my face, something which only members of my own family could do because I was now so tall.

"Hi," I said, "You got the right person?" I didn't think she could want to talk to me. From her well made-up face and nice clothes, she was definitely out of my league. But I was curious about her scissors and why they were pointing at me.

"Oh," she said, noticing my glance at her weapon, "I ran from that hair salon, over there."

"Okay." I was still not sure what her race was about.

"I see yuh every day, walking past my salon," she said. "And you're always too far away for me to talk to yuh. Ah coach models for fashion shows I do every year. You would be just perfect for the styles ah have in mind. Yuh interested in that sort of thing?"

"I, I don't know. I mean . . . I've never modelled before or anything."

"Ah know ah caught you by surprise, but I can assure you, you were created for the catwalk."

"Yuh sure?"

"Yuh have to ask?" Come in and see me soon. Ah got a very early client and am right in the middle of cutting her hair."

She went as quickly as she came and before I turned away, I knew I *would* go see her.

This was the day I was having my interview for the typing school I was going to attend.

I intended to find a job the second I was of age, and if employment was going to come quickly in this town, I needed some typing skills fast. The only problem was, I didn't know how I would pay for it.

The governess' secretary had left me steaming in her office. I wiped my sweaty palms on the sides of the upholstered chair in which I sat. I'd heard the legend of the governess' reign and her attachment to expulsion as the first – not last resort.

"Sorry I'm late," was the first thing the governess said to me. She was much shorter and rounder than my grandmother was, but her back and neck were just as stiff. "I'm short of staff at the moment."

She dropped a large green folder on her desk and took her seat, a great majestic greenheart chair behind the hectic desk. Without asking my name, she fired questions like she was wearing a machine gun on her face. My grandmother's shoulders softened a little when she was talking to someone who was well versed in buttering them up. Anyone who told her of her youthful looks or wisdom was able to lower her lifted nose inch by granite inch.

I didn't know how to use butter very well, but this was a good enough place to start. I shielded each question with a buttered-on-both-sides answer.

"The fee . . ." I began hesitantly, "Is it all payable in advance?"

"Half of it is!" she told me. "You see, we pride ourselves in the students we take. This institution doesn't do failure. We have the British standards to upkeep! They still mark our exam papers. First, we sift our girls well so we're sure they can do the work. Secondly," the governess counted off three fingers when she said, 'secondly.' I figured this meant she either wasn't paying full attention, or she had something else to list but wasn't going to add it at this time.

"Secondly, we take part of the payment up-front to make sure they won't just quit. If you want to do Typing and Advanced English, we need some of *both* fees upfront."

"It's just that I've started taking University classes and . . ."

My heart was sinking fast. I was hoping we'd be allowed to pay in little instalments. This would give me time to find cleaning work or something while I waited to be the right age to start working.

"University classes, you said? What are you studying?"

"Child Psychology."

"Fantastic. Working hard?"

"Always. I would work even harder if I could get some type of part-time job."

"Not in this town, girl. Not at your age."

"I really want to do the Typing and Advanced English," I told her, "But we can't afford the down-payment, even for Typing on its own."

I didn't get up to leave. I waited for her to tell me to.

"Tell you what," she said, "My English teacher has just left the country, which means I have more work than I can handle – not to mention all this paperwork." The governess patted a bunch of files piled on her desk.

"You got good grades in English. You speak very well. Teach my Elementary English class!"

"What?"

"Right place, right time and all that. Teach my Elementary English class. You teach this class, and do your Typing and Advanced English and we're even. Nobody owes anybody.

"Well."

"You in or not? I have things to do."

"Yes. Yes, I'm in!" I answered.

"See you in September," she said, and got up to leave, perhaps to do more work than she could handle. She left me to see myself out.

I savoured her plush office for another second or two, staring at the picture of the Comrade Leader on the wall. I bet he didn't teach English at a quasi-posh British-run typing school.

CHAPTER 19 – COMRADE LEADER

"We regret to inform you of the passing of his Excellency, President Linden Forbes Sampson Burnham."

A song was playing on the radio and suddenly, it wasn't. There was a moment of white noise, as if the announcer couldn't believe what he had been told to say. His normally calm voice sounded like a man ordering his last meal before his execution.

I was sitting on one of the two chairs we possessed, doing some coursework, and waiting for Razor's show to start. He also worked as a Music Promoter and had been off air for a while. I was hoping he was returning with some fresh news about my favourite artistes.

The air outside seemed still, as if all the birds and stray animals – even Miss Hyacinth's chickens – were listening to find out how the announcer was going to be punished for the sick joke he'd just pulled. Would he be shot in the face during a pretend car accident? Would his house be burnt to the ground, leaving no survivors? Or would he be lucky enough to be boated out to Suriname under the sagging canopy of night?

Comrade Leaders like Burnham didn't die. They live on forever, don't they? In all my life living as one of 'Burnham's Children,' I never thought he *could* die.

We would *always* spend hours in the food lines hanging around for rationed food. Wheat flour would *always* be a thing of the past. It would *always* be difficult to leave the country, and his never-aging face and blue dashiki would forever adorn the schools and public buildings.

How could someone so powerful, someone who commanded so much fear even *become* ill? In my wildest possibilities – and I had some 'out-there' stuff going on in my head – the Comrade Leader dying was never one of them.

I felt nothing for him, so my panic was confusing. What was going to happen? Whose child would I be? I felt like I should look outside to see if the world had changed, because my earth felt heavily shifted.

It seemed like overnight before all the banned stuff flooded back to the shelves. This didn't make it easier for my family to get food, but at least the food was there for people who had money to get it.

The speed of the whole operation gave me the image of the banned stuff in a huge warehouse, whose fantastically great doors were half-open. As soon as Burnham died, everything was hustled out to the shops in giant lorries, at top-speed – just in case he returned and made us burn them all on a big pyre.

Before long, I saw that the school kids had changed back to their schools' original uniforms – the ones we wore before we were made to dress identically.

***

My university classes and working, slash studying at the Typing school took a lot of my time. Mum was working hard, paying for our lives, and Franc had made several friends in the street, but I was yet to do so.

Legion of Mary meetings and visits to homes, the Orphanage and the *Old Folks Home* kept me busy most evenings. So when Brian and Dave said I should join the Church choir, I wasn't too keen at first.

They'd obviously never listened to my mediocre renditions of the pop songs I heard on Razor Da Silva's big show.

On Saturday, I went along to the choir practice, anyway. The choir's two guitarists were demonstrating some chords while we hung around under Father's house.

"You children had yuh party here last weekend," a familiar voice shouted. TNM, so full of curiosity, couldn't wait until she was inside the gate to start her lecture.

"Ah don't know why Father put up with yuh all," she continued, walking closer to where the group of us were sitting on chairs and hanging round the ping-pong table, "And all the nonsense yuh get up to."

"Yes, Miss T." Dave said.

"What's that?" TNM turned around to face him. She didn't know our nickname for her. I poked him in the back and he coughed.

"Just some T in me throat." He coughed some more – a bit hacking this time. "There! Got that T!"

"Yuh all had any alcohol at the party?" she asked, continuing to lay the eyes-over-glasses guilt stare on our group. Jay, one of the guitar players had resumed his guitar-playing and some of the others were going back to their game.

"Only what we thought won't affect the price of sugar," Dave answered. A few of us nearby couldn't hold in our laughter.

"No, we didn't have any alcohol. Most of us don't even drink," someone else said.

"Well . . . yes," TNM stuttered a bit. She wasn't expecting that answer. "I would throw the lot of yuh out if ah was he," she said, pointing up to where the priest was probably taking his hundredth enforced nap of the day (due to something resembling narcolepsy).

"Keep the pressure on, Miss T. The youths of today, right?" Dave continued – with another poke in the back from me.

"Is Father upstairs?" she said at last, so angry, she stomped her foot. No one answered, and she walked away to find out for herself.

"You shouldn't trust him, Miss T."

"What?" she asked, turning around swiftly. It took her maybe a full second to realise that she *Trusts No Man*. This time she did hear Dave call her Miss T, but didn't ask why.

"She's a nice lady," I said when she was out of earshot. "You didn't have to be so mean."

"Mean? Who was mean?"

"Back to your guitar lesson, Anne," Brian, came over and whispered, "Yuh got both of them fighting to teach *just* you."

"I thought *Dave* was the funny one," I said.

"Funny? There's other people learning, and both of them sitting by you, showing yuh the same thing."

"Just co-incidence," I laughed. "I can't stay anyway. I got a fashion show tonight.

CHAPTER 20 – THE FASHION SHOW

My father was transferred to Linden – a town far away and difficult to get to. He seemed happy to go and took his kids with him.

I knew from experience that if it involved any effort on his part, I wouldn't see him again for a while. And I wasn't wrong. The sad thing was, I wasn't going to see Sue or my other siblings either.

I told him about typing school and my University classes. I thought he would ask how we were paying for them, but I guess he'd long made up his mind that he was *not* responsible for me or for anything I did.

I couldn't *wait* for the day when I no longer cared whether he loved me or not.

Before he left, he took me to his friend's retirement party, where he waltzed with me. So at least I can say I was *close* to him – once.

It was a little past midnight. Mum was at work, and Franc and I had just made a triumphant journey back home.

My most recent fashion show had made me sufficient money to get her some new school uniforms, shoes and a school bag – and that was enough.

Tonight's bizarre journey was planned earlier this month. After seeing me in my first show, a boutique owner and Show Promoter asked me to make a guest appearance in a fashion show he was holding in a nearby town. He would pick me up in his car at eight in the evening, from the nicer end of my street, and together we would travel to the show.

I happily agreed to do it because we needed the money. Mum was taking days off work and was able to work less and less.

Something in the Show Promoter's body language was nagging me, though, so I wracked my brain of how I could build a back-up strategy.

I found it suspicious that his stylists didn't ask for my size, or that I hadn't been fitted for any of the dresses I was supposed to wear. The only safety net I had was my little sister, so I made a last-minute plan when the day finally arrived.

"We're going for a long drive to Rosehall, I told her earlier in the afternoon."

"Yeah!" she screamed. I was almost sure she hadn't driven in a car for years.

"You excited?"

"Yeah. Who we going with?"

"Just a friend," I said. "If ah have to model, you'll get to sit at the front and watch the show!"

"Yuh got nice clothes to wear?"

"Yep. Put your cat-suit on, right? If they take pictures, you can be in them." (The only nice outfit Franc had was a cat suit I'd gone everywhere in when it used to fit me).

I got us some dinner; we carried the water we needed for our wash in Miss Hyacinth's lean-to kitchen; then we walked in the dark, dodging the waterlogged manholes, to the end of the street, where Mr. Promoter was going to pick me up.

The first thing he said, when he drove up in his fancy car was, "Yuh dint have to have someone wait with yuh, did yuh? You a big girl."

"She's not *just* waiting. She's coming with me." I watched his face and his shoulders and thought I saw the latter rise a bit.

"Oh . . . but she'll get in the way," he stuttered at last, but didn't attempt to drive off.

"No," I replied. "She's good and will do what she's told." I noticed something in his face but didn't understand until later, after I beat him at his game, that it was anger – or maybe even panic.

I sat in the front seat with him, and Franc got in the back. We made small talk and eventually got to Rosehall town, where the fashion show was supposed to have been in full swing. But he drove on, and it didn't take him long to drive right out of town.

"Isn't this Rosehall?" I enquired, as the road sign said we'd left the town and entered another.

"Yeah . . . is just, ah made a mistake with the address . . . is just two minutes up the road," he said as we continued. Two towns later, I realised that he was looking out for something.

"What are you looking for?" I asked, edging out of *concerned* into *worry*. By this time he was sweating like a hog in a sheet, and had opened his side of the car window to let some of the humid night air in.

The stars, by now, were shimmering full-strength. And with the moon moving just overhead, the night had become quite bright. Three villages on and we still hadn't 'found' the fashion show. He stopped a couple of times at village halls where the lights were on and there were people milling around. It occurred to me that he was looking for anything, any meeting of more than a few people that he could pretend was a fashion show. He desperately didn't want to be found out to be a liar.

Unfortunately for him that night, there was no such thing on. He pulled up at one event where people seemed to be leaving an Indian wedding. "Is it there?" he asked quietly.

I felt anger boiling up inside me. I was fuming, not because he couldn't *find* 'the fashion show' but because he thought so little of me – just another young girl in the town, whom he could take out for a drive behind his wife's back. Then what? Then what?

And what would've happened if I said no, or had he never been told that?

"So you don't really know where this show is and you're promoting it?" I asked. Despite my anger, I didn't want to burn any bridges if they really *were* bridges.

Eventually we came to a fairground, and Mr. Promoter said, "Is here! Is here! All'yuh wait here and lemme go in and see."

Maybe in his panic, he didn't see the signs that clearly said '*Fair!*' with *no* mention of what was supposed to be a big fashion show.

As I watch him walk in, I realised that there was no bridge – not this time. There was no fashion show, there never was! Promoter had panicked when he saw the little girl standing beside me on the road.

From the window of his car, I could see him walking around in the light of the fair. Maybe the coward even had to pay to get in. Didn't he know I could see him?

I suddenly felt extremely bold, like I was unexpectedly empowered with the self-respect he dropped on his way out of the car.

"They cancelled the show. They got the fair instead," he said, and got back into the car. I didn't bother to ask how the he, the Promoter, could convert his fashion show audience into revellers at a fair while driving his car aimlessly around, or how they managed to rig up fairground rides and music in a couple of hours. My newfound strength assured me I didn't need all the answers.

Tonight I was able to allow the poop to pass me by without having to feel around in there for all the sweet-corn detail.

I caught myself embarrassed for him and quickly hardened my heart.

He turned the car around, and finally we were heading home. I thought about all my friends tucked up safely in their beds and wondered why my life couldn't be like theirs. Maybe modelling wasn't such a good idea for me. I probably couldn't make as much money as we needed, and if Mr. Coward was anything to go by, people think you're someone you're not.

"What did you think would happen tonight?" I asked, trying to keep the bitterness I felt inside from creeping up to my voice. I was aware of the little girl sitting in the back seat and didn't want to drop her into the same pot of mess I lived in when I was her age. She would be kept safe.

"What yuh mean?"

"I mean was there *ever* a fashion show?"

"Yuh a bold girl, you know."

"You think I'm bold?" I asked. "Well I'll take that. But you throw it out like it's such a bad thing."

"Girls like yuh shouldn't talk to people like that!"

"Girls like me? I'm young and pretty and I got no one to protect or look out for me. It's girls like me who *should* be bold. We have to do *everything* to protect ourselves!"

I looked across at his double chin and it occurred to me for the first time how ugly he really was. Maybe I was finally seeing his ugly reflection manifested on his face. I opened my mouth to tell him of his ugliness and closed it again. It was nearly eleven o'clock. This was late in these parts and we had absolutely no one to call if he told us to get out of his car. I had to make sure he took us back home.

"You tink yuh pretty?"

"Yes. I don't think I would be here – in your car, if I weren't."

He didn't argue with this. He mumbled something under his breath about pride, then stopped flopping his stupid chins about. If only he knew how hard I'd worked on the inside – for years – to come to that conclusion!

Finally, he dropped us off where he'd picked us up. He didn't even offer to take us back home, but that was okay. Maybe the coward didn't want to be seen with two young girls whose collective ages were probably half his own. As I stepped out of the car, I opened my mouth again to tell him he was ugly, but couldn't do it. It would hurt his feelings too deeply.

As soon as he drove away, I felt my new-found power rise in me again. I wouldn't let the breakers win. If they were smart, I had to be smarter. I would stick a screwdriver into their nicely carved sinister confidence and chip away at them little by little. I knew I didn't have to touch or say anything to them. All I had to do was show them they couldn't break *one* girl – *just* one. Any *one* would do.

"That man take us for a nice ride, Anne." Franc said. "The back seat was really nice."

"Hmm," I replied. "I bet you couldn't see as much as I could from the front." I put my hand around her little shoulders and said to her, "You know what? We did good tonight."

"We did good?" she asked.

"Yep, we did good!" I put my hand up for a high five and she slapped my palm hard. If Miss Bessy's sons had seen us, they would've spread the news all through the street by the next morning. '*That tall, hoity-toity one was high-fiving she sister last night. What they got to high-five about? What* she *got to high-five about? Look where they live, look what they wear – and* she *think she better than we . . . .*'

CHAPTER 21 – MY SIXTEENTH

By this time, I had done a couple of genuine fashion shows. I didn't make the kind of money I heard cat-walk models made in England. I mean, we sometimes had to paint the catwalk ourselves!

I was also promised a temporary job after I turned sixteen. I would do light office work. This would come in handy because Mum was not very well. She was mostly sad than ill, but I couldn't understand why. She had us and we had her, didn't we? She had to go into hospital for surgery on her heel, but I couldn't visit her. I had to take care of Franc.

One of Miss Bessy's daughters had just given birth to a baby who she took for a walk in her arms every morning, up and down the street. Early morning sunshine was good for infants, we were told.

On my birthday, I saw Miss Bessy's daughter coming towards me in the street as I walked home from Mass. Her baby always wore a giant tikka in the middle of her little forehead.

I was very familiar with tikkas. When Franc was a baby, on rare occasions when my grandmother took us out (when we lived with her), she didn't leave the house unless the baby was wearing one.

She looked on as Theresa carefully used a matchstick to take some soot from under the pot. We always had plenty of soot, as our kerosene stove either blazed or went on strike. The flames had to be watched constantly and turned up very high, especially with the makeshift wicks we used.

Theresa rubbed the white end of the matchstick lightly under a pot, removing a spot of black. With the sulphur end facing out, she dotted the matchstick on Franc's forehead.

Franc was a pro at dodging tikkas and ended up with black lines, shapes, zigzags – anything but *dots* – all over her face.

My grandmother used to say she was the worst baby ever for putting on tikkas. As soon as she saw the matchstick, she shook her head from side to side. She even attempted to eat them sometimes, anything but get a tikka!

Tikkas were traditionally a Hindu custom, and they were supposed to deflect the 'bad eye' from people who were jealous of you or your baby.

Miss Bessy's daughter was a lover of tikkas. And she never allowed her baby to face Misha's direction. Misha was one of our few child-less neighbours of baby-bearing age.

As Miss Bessy's daughter passed Misha's house, which was two doors from Leroy's, she turned her baby to face the opposite direction. If I believed in tikkas and bad eyes (and had a baby), I would've turned my baby's head *before* I left home, rather than aggravate my neighbour.

Misha was sitting outside having breakfast on her veranda as usual, watching the school kids go by. She had a particular way of gumming her slices of bread into submission, because her teeth had jumped up and waved goodbye years ago. I took a sly glance at her gum-action every morning when I passed her house.

I guess the regular baby-head-turning had become a bit too much for Misha because she called out to Miss Bessy's daughter.

"Who yuh tink yuh are, eh?" Misha asked. "Yuh tink yuh better than me, no. Well ah tell yuh something, yuh not . . . "

I don't know what else she was going to say, but Miss Bessy's daughter eagerly butted in.

"Yuh can't be talking to me, yuh no-teeth bengelay. Yuh just jealous cos yuh barren!"

Her last sentence made Misha's arms stiffen with anger. She flew down the steps in a rage, and ran up to Miss Bessy's daughter, waving her fingers in her face.

"Chil'ren, or not, at least *I* know who me chil'ren father will be!" Misha shouted.

Even *I* knew that they'd *both* hit each other's rawest joints. In news downtime, the gossips in the street had designated mini-bulletins for all of us. The two ladies hadn't beaten around the bush. They'd both scrambled in there and had worked up friction so sizzling, the bush was blazing!

It was Miss Bessy's daughter's turn to boil. She was so furious, for a moment I thought she was going to throw her baby to the ground, and skin Misha with her bare hands.

Even in the early hours, a small crowd had started to gather. Leroy ran out of his house wearing a bath towel around his chest. He'd stuck it in like a woman tucks her towel over her breasts.

His arms were up, his palms facing front. "Hi," he said, nodding to me and laughing conspiratorially.

"Now, girlth," he said then swallowed with a *ta*. "Ain't it too early to fight?"

"She's *your* friend!" Misha shouted. Miss Bessy's entire family buddied with Leroy (who in their right mind wouldn't? He had some good stuff coming out of his kitchen). They lived across the road from each other and when Miss Bessy ran out of sugar or rice, Leroy was the person the grandkids went to ask, with their enamel cup in hand.

Sometimes the family even popped over to his house to use his toilet when theirs was busy. This was clear when they ran across the road clutching wet pieces of old newspaper. When they got cut short, they hurried over, wrapped in their towels – or sometimes in their bras and half-slips.

Before I could do a double-take, Miss Bessy's daughter was handing the baby to Leroy and diving for pint-sized Misha.

I suppose Misha thought she had the upper hand since her opponent was holding a baby. But Miss Bessy's daughter was on top of her and ripping her clothes off before she had time to react.

I was magically transfixed as Misha, like a little mutt, managed to squirm and wriggle her way on top of Miss Bessy's daughter. She punched and pulled anything not pinned down by skin.

This was when Leroy decided it was time to jump in, and tucked the baby into my hands. As he bent over to pull the two women apart, his towel fell and his chest was laid bare. He was wearing perfectly normal shorts under there.

Leroy ripped Misha off Miss Bessy's daughter. I never found out what he was going to do with her because Jerry Saunders came up, on his way to work and shouted at the group of them. I handed the baby over to Leroy and hurried home. I was angry at myself for stopping, and didn't want to hear what was going to happen next. Jerry Saunders seemed to have Leroy on some kind of leash that no one else could ever find.

About a month later, Misha decided she was pregnant and told everyone in the street to pass it on. *Misha preggers, pass it on. Misha having twins, pass it on. Misha had an abortion, pass it on. Misha boyfriend found out he's sterile, pass it on. Misha up the duff, pass it on.*

About nine months later, nearly ten years after she and her boyfriend got together, Misha had a baby boy. Seems like if you were desperate for a baby, all you had to do was pick a fight with a woman who had a young 'un. Just make sure she didn't call you a *no teeth bengelay*, though.

Three months after her baby was born, Misha decided she was expecting again. Pass it on. *Misha's caught again, pass it on. Misha cooking a bun in de oven, pass it on . . .*

Moira came over in the afternoon to see me.

"Yuh need some fun, girl," she said.

"Ah hear *that* stuff is overrated," I told her.

"But it's yuh birthday. Come on! Ah taking you to Lim Chan's for dinner. Where's yuh sister?"

"Spending the night with some friends. Mum's at work."

"So what yuh say? Going?"

"Yes. It's my birthday. Why not!"

We spent a long time catching up. Rob, the Inspector was out of her life, and she was to leave the country soon.

"So what's going on with you?" she asked. "Seeing anyone?

"No. I'm talking to Sam, but ah don't know . . ."

"Yuh think it could turn into something? Yuh want it to?"

"Not sure. It's not as defined as that. I'm scared to like him more than *he* likes me, and he hasn't said he likes me, so . . ."

"What yuh like about him?"

"He's decent, doesn't swear, and speaks well. Sounds intelligent. Plus, he's tall and good-looking."

"Well, it's still early days," Moira said. "Wait and see, right?"

"Yep. Wait and see. Dunno if I'm ready for a boyfriend, to be honest."

"Let's share a bubbly," Moira said at last.

"I don't know. I've never had a drink before – apart from tasting rum when I was little."

"I'll order a small one and we'll split it. It's got a nice taste. You'll like it."

"How big is the small bottle?"

"It's 350 ml, something like that."

"Okay! It's ma birthday!"

"It's yuh birthday!"

"And it's the closest thing ah will have to a party," I added. "Will it burn my throat? Rum burns your throat, you know."

"No, it tastes good, mon."

It wasn't until I stood up sometime later that I felt the effects of my half glass of bubbly. When my legs buckled under me, Moira took my arm to pull me up again, but I fell back down.

"You can't be serious," Moira laughed.

"What's wrong with me, Moira?" I asked looking up to her from the bench of the shabby Chinese Restaurant. I noticed four – or maybe two – flies land on the spinning fly-catcher above my head. They buzzed for a bit, then were still.

"You're drunk!" Moira replied, laughing again. "You're drunk on a few mouthfuls of Bubbly. What's wrong with yuh?"

"Well, don't stand there laughing," I giggled. "Help me up."

Is this how George feels? Was the first thought that came to mind. Why does he do it over and over again, then? Is he crazy? I used to think he drank a whole lot to get drunk, but if this is all it took, my goodness, was I wrong about him!

"My feet won't walk," I said.

"You're drunk, that's why," Moira laughed again. "I don't *believe* this. Let me help you."

I wouldn't have gotten home if Moira didn't have her bike. I only had one thought in my head as we rode home. I prayed that no one stopped us to talk, especially the parents who'd just asked me to be god-mother for their child.

I made an effort not to stumble, as I walked through the front yard. I barely got in the door before my knees gave way entirely. In the dark, I crawled on my hands and knees into bed. What a rotten way to spend my birthday! I never wanted to feel so out of control ever again. "Bad bubbly," I whispered to myself. And I never touched it again.

CHAPTER 22 – DANCING THE NIGHT AWAY

I'd met Sam just before I turned sixteen. I mean, I had known him for a while because he was a member of our church. He came sporadically and during Lent or Advent.

I couldn't say he was my boyfriend. He occasionally walked me home after Typing school. And we sometimes talked after evening Mass when I passed by the large stone on the side of the road where he met his friends for their evening 'lime.'

I knew he would be too embarrassed to be seen with me for anything more than casual friendship. He was a nice guy, but moved in different circles. He was muscular and lifted weights, but I suspected his kind of strength wasn't strong enough for any type of mould-breaking.

We recently met George's son. George is a drunk and his son Errol never touches liquor. When my psychology teacher preaches about children growing up to do the things they've experienced, I stand up to her. I'd already decided I wouldn't grow up to be like my grandmother, but I hide this from her – well, I hide my past from everyone! But I tell her about twenty-year-old Errol.

Errol told me he grew up in the midst of his parents' fighting, and how his father behaved like a child when he was drunk. I found out that

George didn't get drunk on *just* half a glass of bubbly. He swallowed bottle after bottle of rum.

"Daddy made we go 'ungry, cos he stole the 'ouse money, just so 'e could get rum," Errol said. Country living and school absences had softened Errol's Hs to such an extent they were usually silent.

Errol had left his mother's house in the country to stay with Miss Hyacinth so he could work in our town. He'd found a job at Haven, the biggest restaurant, disco and hotel around.

Errol spent his nights on a roll-out mattress on Miss Hyacinth's floor, and his days and evenings labouring. He was saving up for his wedding because his parents said it was time for him to find a wife.

"So, let me get this straight," I said to him. "You haven't actually found a wife yet."

"No, not yet."

"But you're working long hours to save up for a wedding you don't know will take place."

"Well," he said. "Me already h'old for an Indian bwoy. Ah can't stay on the shelf, mon." Errol made up for his missing Hs by adding them randomly to words beginning with O.

"Why don't you save up for your own place?" I asked. "You stay with us in the daytime and go upstairs to sleep. You will really need somewhere to *actually* live when you get married."

"Too many questions, mon," he said, pretending to be angry, but Errol was a teddy bear. "Ah can stay with me mother in she 'ouse, or ah can stay with me wife's parents."

"The wife you don't know yet."

"Stop it."

"Dave and his sisters invited me to go dancing tonight at the Haven," I said at last. "We're coming over about 9 o'clock. You gonna be there?"

"Yeah. Ah working tonight, but ah gon be at the back scrubbing on me knees, while you rich and famous dance the night away."

The first time Dave's sisters invited me to a party, I wasn't sure that Mum would let me go. I didn't have anything to wear, and certainly didn't have any extra money to take 'the nibbles' they recommended.

Mum said I was old enough to go, Sash lent me her maxi dress, which was just about right for me, and Dave promised to bring my portion of the nib-nibs. Before long, we were going dancing regularly, and I was dancing away my inhibitions all night. The more I danced, the surer I became of me. I realised this town was not where I was supposed to be. I was certain I would dance my way right out of it before long.

"How come you dance like that without a drink?" Dave's older sister asked. "I gotta have something to keep me going, if you know what I mean."

I thought of the bubbly and shook the image of me stumbling to bed – in the dark – out of my head. "Music gets me tipsy," I laughed. While dancing, I was a free teenager. I wore no shackles; bore no burdens.

"Do you drink *anything* at all? Don't you get thirsty?"

"I have an orange juice sometimes," I answered. But what I didn't say was that I drank my saliva most times to wet my throat. Dave always paid for my ticket into the hall and I couldn't let him buy me juice was well. I was now doing office work part-time while studying. Mum was also working part-time, which meant that together we could barely eat, live and keep Franc in school.

One Saturday night I felt a tap on my shoulder, and someone whispered 'Annabella' in my ear. Solly was standing behind me with two beers in his hand.

"What you doin' here?" I shouted.

"Me and Lisa come here regular. She sitting right there." Solly pointed to a table in the far corner of the darkened room. I waved at Lisa, but she didn't see me.

"Come over," Solly said. He went back to the bar and got me a Pepsi.

I chatted with Lisa for a while, then Solly took her hand and asked her to dance.

"Ah really tired, Sol," Lisa said. "Lemme finish me beer!"

"But this is my favourite number!"

"They *all* yuh favourite, Solsol. Go dance with Anne."

"Annabella, you game? Solly asked.

"I'm new to this, and ah not really good at waltzing," I told him.

"Let him teach yuh, girl. He's the best. Really," Lisa said.

"Okay," I said, and Lisa leaned back in her chair and stretched her legs out in front of her.

And there began my waltz lessons. I had only Brian, Dave and some other friends from whom to judge, but by their standards, Solly was king. He moved with the grace of a man half *my* weight.

For the first time in my life, I felt protected. Solly held me with firmness, but his hand on my back and the one holding mine were soft and gentle.

With him I knew I was respected. I was a princess and he was my father, the king. For the first time since dancing with my own father, I was dancing with someone as tall as myself. Solly gave freely, of everything he offered, but would never require payment – of any sort. Song after song, we waltzed and Lisa, legs stretched out, looked on.

CHAPTER 23 – THE JOB

I finally found a permanent job after graduating Typing school. I was the secretary and office manager of an auto shop, where they repaired cars and sold spare parts. I did the accounts, dealt with customers, took care of the shop and basically did everything that wasn't hands-on car work.

It was a small town, so naturally my boss was someone whose works everyone was familiar with. True to trend, his name isn't just, Matt. It's always, *Matt Peters*.

I was dumped on my butt, in the middle of a lion's den working for him, but there were no jobs going in town. Matt Peters was a part of Jerry Saunders' circle of ~~fiends~~ friends.

I knew who he was when I went to work for him, but since Mum was no longer working, I needed a job that covered most of our needs. Besides, ugly Mr. Promoter had taught me it was possible to beat them at their game – *just one girl*.

If I worked really hard, I could change things for us. Maybe we could find a bigger, nicer place and I could buy better clothes for us. My last show paid for two working outfits, but as life didn't offer me the time to do part-time work, I'd have to do my shows as paying hobbies.

When I found permanent work, I had two choices: live my own life and keep my earnings for myself, or become the parent and sole breadwinner – taking care of the rent and bills, and keeping my sister in school. I did what anyone else would do.

After all, what chance did my little sister have of staying in school or even staying *alive* if I left. The time had come for *me* to save somebody. I was living on Payback Street.

So this is how, at nearly seventeen, I began to make all the major decisions for my little family. Mum lobbed the ball over, and I caught and carried it in both hands. I'd been prepared for its descent for some time, so I was hanging around nearby when it became airborne.

Matt Peters was married. However, when it came to womanizing, Jerry Saunders was playing high school football, and he was in a Premiership team.

Just two weeks after I started working for Matt Peters, an old school friend, H caught me on the way back from work one evening as I passed my grandmother's house, deliberately walking on the other side of the road. H said she wanted to chat with me the following day. This was unusual, since we'd stopped catching up with each other lately.

H and I met in a café and bought ourselves a couple of Pepsis. It was the first time in my entire life, I could afford to take spare change out of my purse to buy myself a drink.

"The reason ah telling yuh," she began, once we got the pleasantries out of the way, "Is because now that yuh working with Matt Peters, yuh sure to find out."

"Find out what?"

"So you and Matt Peters together?" she answered my question with one of her own.

"What? He's married, girl! Besides, I find him repulsive." I laughed, desperately hoping she was joking. Matt Peters was a heavy-set man in his late thirties. He always dressed well – too well for a mechanic. He smelled nice, but even his perfume had a whiff of something that wasn't quite right. Maybe I was the only one who smelled the deceitful version of Matt Peters. The smell got even worse after he tried talking me up, but by then his scent was a nauseating *odour* to me.

"I don't like bad-boys, H. You know that by now. And he still fancies himself a *boy*. I'll give him the *bad* part, though," I laughed. "*Bad* as in rotten, gone-over, spoilt."

"You don't find bad boys at least, a bit exciting?"

"No. The clue's in the name. Bad boys treat you bad. I want to be treated well. Bad boys are up themselves and have personality disorders that make them suck happiness out of women's pain."

"Me and Jerry Saunders . . ." H blurted out. "Ah know Matt Peters will tell you and ah wanted you to hear my side first."

I was shocked for two reasons: H was not the type. She was from a good family, and in our town, this was weighed in gold. Secondly, she told me – but why? What did it have to do with me and how was it my business?

"It just happened and now he won't see me. Ah getting married to go abroad anyway, so it don't matter now," H continued, taking a big gulp of her Pepsi.

"Ah used to come to his house, but we used to check that you weren't around first, though." I couldn't help wondering if this was her idea or his.

"He didn't say," was all I could manage.

"Me brother knows someone who's coming to marry me," H said.

"Is he nice?" I asked.

"Ah only seen a picture of him, he looks nice."

As I walked home, I tried to work out how long it would be before I lost the next person I've treasured in my life. If I could, I'd build a mansion and make special rooms for each of my flesh-treasures so they didn't see the need to leave me.

A Guyanese Proverb: Rain ah fall, bukit na full, dew caan full am.

Translation: If rain can't fill the bucket, dew won't fill it.

Meaning: if you want something that requires a lot of energy, don't think that you can achieve it by doing less than necessary.

CHAPTER 24 – PLAYING THE PART

"I got two lines!" I ran into our house shouting and waving my script over my head. My old English teacher, Mr. Pegg had recently come back to town. He'd gone off to study when I was in my first year of high school.

Now he was back, and was a playwright and director! I'd heard he was looking for actors for his new play but by the time I'd worked up enough courage to approach him in the street, most of the roles had been taken.

I eventually auditioned, and got a part with two lines. *Two lines for my debut performance!* I repeated to myself all day long. Even the guilt I felt for feeling so proud of myself couldn't dampen my spirits. I couldn't speak for *myself* a few years ago, and now I was going to speak to the town! I was so happy I felt I would burst. All rehearsals were late evening, so work and classes never clashed.

Two days later at rehearsals, we were going full steam inside the G.T.U hall. I'd joined the play two weeks after everyone else and had to do some hard running to catch up.

"I want you to leave the house," Maria the main character (played by Mr. Pegg's relative) was saying to her husband.

I gazed at Lisa, the actress, as I waited – scene after scene, for my part to come around. Lisa was in every scene, digging her teeth into the juiciest part of the play. She would later stand a real stage trial and be found guilty of murdering her abusive husband. She was going to have to bring on the tears – in front of the entire town!

"No, Lisa," Mr Pegg said, and he repeated the line for the third time in the way he had written it to be said.

"I want you to leave the *house*," Lisa repeated. Mr Pegg walked away with his head in his hands.

The rest of us fell silent. Of the *many* people auditioning for the play, we were the ones he picked. We didn't want to put a foot wrong in case we all got the boot.

I sat on the floor to appear as small as possible. I knew I would be the first one out if he decided to get rid of us all. After all, I had the audacity to confront him in the street.

But the power I once felt to beat Mr. Promoter was bubbling up inside me again. Before I knew I'd opened my mouth, I was screaming, with a tremor in my voice, "I want you to leave the house!"

Lisa and two of the other actors were standing on the very stage Burnham graced once, perhaps in the very spot. She stared open-mouthed at me and I stopped breathing.

"That's it!" Mr Pegg shouted. "Anne, do the rest of the page." He pointed me to the stage. At the end of the page, he nodded for me to go on.

"At last!" Mr. Pegg shouted, when we read the pages and I found the tears Maria needed to shed. "I've found someone who can cry *actual* tears!"

I didn't tell him, but the tears of the made-up Maria, were very real within me, and I had a lot more where those had come from. I came home that night still shaking, for I had returned with dozens of pages of new lines to learn. I was Maria! And Maria had lines on each page of the lengthy script.

This was the first of several lead roles, of many plays in my town and even at the biggest playhouse in the entire country! But by then I was another person, one who had learned to recognise the tricks of Mr. Promoter and had beaten him, Jerry Saunders, Matt Peters and his side-kick when they tried to break me.

Errol found his wife before Solly's brother's wedding. Unlike Solly's family, Errol had no elaborate party planned. No family members were flying in from Canada, and no expensive decorations were being shipped.

Errol brought his new wife from his new home across the river, to show her off to us. They both lived with her parents, and her brother and sister, and Errol was now looking for a new job nearby.

Like clockwork, every Saturday he and his wife visited us. We now had enough to eat and even a couple of spare plates to share some lunch with them.

At the end of the third month, after visiting us every Saturday, Errol missed a week.

"Where's Errol?" I asked George, after he stirred red-eyed about midday. Mum was at the market shopping and I was doing our washing in a big basin by the back door. Franc had already gone out for a game of hopscotch in the street.

"Ah don't want to talk 'bout that boy," George answered.

"Please tell me he's okay! He found a job or something? Something wrong with his wife?"

"He alright," was all George said and walked heavily up Miss Hyacinth's stairs.

The next Saturday, Errol brought us a surprise. He visited with a different girl, who he introduced as his wife's sister.

"Sharma not feeling too well," he told me when I asked after his wife. His sister-in-law was pleasant enough, but it took me about four-weeks' worth of sister-in-law visits to realise that Errol was no longer with his wife but with her *sister*.

He practically lived with us, yet we didn't know him. What on earth blinded us to this side of him?

His story reminded me of Devika's (one of my goddaughters) situation, and I dread the outcome of his life, because this last year was hell for Devika's family.

When the family was converted to Catholicism (both parents, she, her sister and a brother), they had to have godparents.

Devika took my name at her confirmation and we became very close. A few months later, her sister got married and moved not too far away. I regularly visited Devika after work, and when she finished her high school exams, she told me she was going to live with her sister to help her take care of her market business and the baby she was expecting.

In a few months, Devika's heavily pregnant sister had moved back home because she, Devika, had taken her husband and was now mistress of her house.

How could I not feel this betrayal in Devika? I was supposed to be her mentor, so how could I not see all this?

If you were sensitive enough to people so close to you, maybe you could say or do something to stop the dreadful hurt they cause other people.

I could never talk to Devika when I saw her in the street, even after she appeared with baby number one, or baby number two.

When I went to the market, I avoided the stall she and her stolen husband ran there. Did I think that what she did was unforgivable? Nothing is unforgivable, but it wasn't me she hurt.

CHAPTER 25 – INSIDE JERRY SAUNDERS' LAIR

I only knew he got me to visit his house under false pretences, once I was already there and seated. But this is how I defeated Jerry Saunders at his own nasty game.

Jerry Saunders met me in the street and told me he'd dubbed me the best cassette he'd made in years.

"What kind of music yuh listen to?" he'd asked a couple of weeks ago.

"Anything, really," I replied. "A lot of sixties music played in the house when I was growing up, so I like oldies. But I love the new, popular stuff as well."

"What? The kind of thing Razor plays on his show?" Jerry Saunders asked.

"Yes. I listen to him every day at work."

"Yuh know, I went to one of his shows in Georgetown."

"Really? I'm impressed! What's he like?"

"He was too far away for me to see clearly," Jerry Saunders replied. "But ah know he's tall. Got dark hair and white skin."

"Did you go up especially for his show, or were you already in the city?" I was genuinely fascinated that Jerry Saunders had seen my favourite radio D.J.

"Ah went up for the show because ah heard he'd won that Caribbean D.J competition thing. Ah knew all the best entertainers would be there, yuh know. Razor got the crowd moving and grooving."

It was a week later when he told me he'd taped music off Razor's show.

"Well, I don't really have a cassette player," I told him, "But I suppose I could borrow Sash's."

"I'll bring over the cassette," he said, but he never did.

A week later, he called out to me as I was passing his house on my way home from classes.

"Hey, Anne! Come up for the cassette." And I did. I did because he'd stopped making passes at me lately. I did because I figured that since I knew about him and H, we had a common secret to keep. Somehow, I felt this made us friends, connected by this confidence.

I knew he hadn't changed because I heard of some of his exploits from his gang-member, my boss. It was becoming increasingly difficult to work in that environment, where daily conversations were about the girls Matt Saunders and his pack of ~~liars~~ lions had hunted – broken, unwrapped. And clearly, they didn't care that I knew some of the girls.

There were only two good things – no, three good things about working at the shop. I got a steady income to run our home; I made a new friend in Clive, the ex-soldier and boxer (Clive worked in the shop repairing cars, but didn't join in Matt Peters' battle-conversations) and I got to listen to Razor even in the blackouts because the shop had a generator.

Clive was trying to set up a meeting with a friend of his, who owned an export business.

"He needs someone confident and trustworthy to work for he," Clive told me. "You'd be just perfect."

I thought Clive was sweet for looking out for me. After all, I'd never even asked him to.

"Yuh just need to get out of this environment," he always said.

"Hi," Jerry Saunders said as I walked upstairs to his room. Leroy still lived downstairs. His place was spacious and squeaky clean. His kitchen was spotless – not a spoon was out of place. The house was once his family home, with the bedrooms upstairs and the living areas downstairs.

It was clear they hadn't done any additional building work on the house to make it into two separate flats. The bedrooms were where they always were and one of them was Jerry Saunders' cave. Jerry Saunders opened his door and beckoned me in.

"Welcome, on your very first visit, to my humble abode."

"You say that like you expect me to come again."

He laughed. I felt uncomfortable, especially since Leroy was nowhere to around. Where was he anyway? He was always pottering about at this time, flouncing around, throwing his hands up in the air, getting his frill on.

"Where's Leroy?" I asked as matter-of-factly as I could. I didn't want him to know I was scared.

"Oh, he had to go to Georgetown for couple 'a days – family stuff," Jerry Saunders replied. He had a large shelf on his wall with various pictures of his son, and no fewer than twenty cassettes. I had never seen so many in my entire life.

"Sit down." He pointed to the bed. There was no other place in the room on which to sit. *Was this the spot where H sat? Why did I have to sit? I was getting my tail out of the door as soon as the cassette was in my hand.*

"Now where is this tape?" He looked around on his shelf and found what he was looking for.

"Oh, thank you," I said, getting up.

"No, sit down," Jerry Saunders said. "Ah want you to listen to it and tell me which ones you like best."

This wasn't what I had in mind at all. This is all going pear-shaped. I wanted to just pick up the tape and leave. I didn't even think I had to climb the stairs. Thoughts were swimming around in my head, and adrenaline gave me a sharp, swift kick in the side.

"This first one, ah know yuh will like," Jerry Saunders said sitting down next to me. He was too calm, too . . . Jerry Saunderish. I shuffled down slightly, so he could have more space. He seemed way too close to me. I'd never sat that close to a man before.

Jerry Saunders was right. *'Careless Whisper'* was my definite favourite of all time.

"So, you have a boyfriend now," he said.

"Not really."

"What does 'not really' mean? I see that tall, mixed-race boy you walk home with sometimes," Jerry Saunders said pouring beer into two glasses, all of which he had on a small stand by his bed. *He had a beer and two glasses upstairs!* Big sirens went off in my head, but I tried to keep calm. He handed one of the glasses to me. *Was he stalking me? I had never seen him seeing Sam.*

"No, thank you," I said, "I don't drink."

"Yuh joking right? Yuh party a lot, don't you? You can't tell me you doan drink when you go partying."

"I dance. If you want to call that partying, well I party, but I don't need alcohol to enjoy myself. I just don't drink."

"Really?"

"Yes. I just want to enjoy it, not get drunk and stuff like that. And you can't enjoy something if you're drunk."

I felt like a mouse cornered by a large cat. I knew if I turned and ran, he was faster than me and I would get caught. I had to stare the cat down, look it in the eyes and work out a technique to back away without it seeing me move. I would try going around in circles, facing my face forward until I worked out my plan. I was going to get out of here whole.

"And yuh boyfriend?" he asked, one eyebrow raised higher than I thought possible. "Does he dance?"

"Sam and I don't really move in the same circles. We're only friends. But yes, he's a really good dancer."

"Same circles, huh. Ah saw him carrying yuh into the yard the other day," Jerry Saunders insisted.

It took me a minute to recall the lifting. "Oh, we were just messing around. Sam enters bodybuilding competitions. He was just pretending to lift me like a bar bell."

Just the thought of it made me smile and relax a bit. Sam could be funny and even spontaneous. Sometimes I thought that he liked me more than he let on, then at other times, I felt as if we were barely associates.

Last weekend I went out to the Haven with Dave and his sisters and a few other friends. Sasha had also recently started coming out with our group.

Sam and his friends also hung out at the Haven because it was the only place in our tiny town we *could* go. So far though, we've never been there together. However, if we ran into each other, we sometimes danced together – if he asked me, as girls never asked boys to dance.

His friends were further up the church-front-seat ladder than Dave and I were. On Saturday, several of us were on the stage dancing together. Sam and I found ourselves back to back to each other, each of us dancing with someone else.

Sam linked his arms with mine, behind his back, as we both danced with our own dance partners. I happened to look to the side of me and saw Aaran's aunt (who came with Sam's group) point to our arms and she, her boyfriend, and the couple next to them laughed.

I knew that look and laugh well. It was the look I got when I wore the same dress over and over and over. I let go of Sam's arms because I felt that *he* would break the link if he saw them laughing. I didn't know for sure, but it felt better not waiting to find out.

"Maybe we should do some playing around like your friend," Jerry Saunders had said but I was hearing him from miles away. His hand found its way onto my lap.

"No, don't!" I snapped. But he pushed me down on the bed and had pinned both my hands down.

I thought about Promoter guy's fat chins and how much I hated them. Something told me that if I got angry with Jerry Saunders it wouldn't end well. I had the feeling he was well versed in this kind of thing; well used to getting his own way.

"Please don't do this," I begged. All the tears I'd found for Maria and the other women I'd played had deserted me. Where were they when I needed them for *me*? Had Maria shed all the tears I had left in me? *Please God, Please God.*

"Ever been kissed?" he asked.

"No. Please."

I could scream. Would it be okay to scream? Would Miss Bessy hear me from across the street? Would she send her son or would she think I was finally getting my comeuppance for ignoring his attempts to chat me up?

The sound of the zipper on the side of my skirt brought me back into the room with a horrible bang. If I didn't stop this now, it would end in disaster for me.

"I have my periods!" I shouted, and he paused.

"What?" His hands stopped moving and I knew I had my chance.

"Yes, it's been really heavy this month. I think I might have a bad kind of problem." I held his eyes with mine. I remembered my Science teacher who saw something in them that made him let go of my hand. Maybe Jerry Saunders would see that same thing, whatever it was. *Please God, Please God.*

"You're so nervous," he muttered, as if he had just lectured me on the movement of bug-life in South America or some such boring topic. Then he let me up. I jumped off the bed, pulled up my zip, and brushed down my hair with my hands. Mum was home and I didn't want to worry her. I would pretend everything was fine.

"You've never done this," he said.

I shook my head, casting my eyes down so he couldn't see the tears, which had finally made their appearance.

"But yuh seventeen with a boyfriend. How come?"

"Not my boyfriend," I muttered. I took a few tiny steps backwards. I still didn't want to make any sudden moves.

"Come and listen to music any time yuh want," Jerry Saunders said to me cheerfully, as I left his room – face forward. He didn't offer me the cassette.

I fled downstairs, wiped my eyes and walked home to help my mum make dinner. I've never told anyone about the incident. I realised as I left his house, that going there was a *very* stupid thing to do.

CHAPTER 26 – MEETING A MAN ABOUT A THING

Errol has visited us with his mother-in-law the last couple of weeks. He and his wife are still legally married, and he's stopped seeing her sister.

This time round, we knew before he told us, that 'mother-in-law' was now 'live-in wife.'

"But I love 'er!" he shouted in my face when I called him aside to ask what was going on.

"How can you, Errol? How *can* you? You lived with us. I thought I knew you. How could you stand to do this kind of thing?"

"Love choose you. Not the h'other way around. Besides, yuh not even 'ave a boyfriend. Yuh don't know stuff."

"I know I have a *choice*, Errol," I answered. "I have a choice to hurt someone or *not* to hurt someone. Is this why her husband committed suicide? Did he find the two of you together?"

"Well, he was depressed. It 'ad nothin' to do with this."

George was so embarrassed by his son, that a little while after Errol came over with his mother-in-law, he moved out of Miss Hyacinth's house.

She soon brought a distant niece to live with her. Gloria sometimes felt the need to undress entirely when coming downstairs for a walk. She'd mislaid her mind a long time ago. They took all her teeth at the mental hospital because she chomped on everyone who tried to treat her.

Old Miss Hyacinth was now left with the task of placing Gloria's tablets in her mouth, then holding her nostrils shut, so she would swallow them.

"Gloria! Gloria! she shouts, "Swallow them now! Lemme see under yuh tongue!"

Gloria was the opposite of my aunt Theresa during her breakdowns. Theresa hugged and kissed everyone in sight. Gloria preferred to hit and spit. I hadn't realised how difficult the latter was without teeth, until I met Gloria. But I suppose it's not one of the things we consider.

I mean, how someone without teeth spits is not a thing you have conversations about. Same as, how does someone with a lisp say the word, *lisp*? And how does a person with dyslexia spell the word? Why do we have to complicate disabilities? I have an uncle who stutters and when he attempts to *talk* about his stutter, he goes, "St . . . st . . . ststst . . . stut . . ." oh! Just forget it!

Gloria added another interesting element to our outside baths, especially when she wakes up before dawn and waits outside our backdoor *after* hiding yesterday's pills under her tongue.

***

Finally, the week of Solly's brother's wedding had arrived. Elaine, Solly's sister, will be moving to Canada after the wedding, and her sister-in-law, Donna and *her* baby will be left in the house. The only brother who was not going to be at the wedding was Donna's husband.

Sometime after the wedding, I again had to worm my way out of another sticky situation. Clive, my ex-soldier friend at work had finally set up the meeting for me with his exporting-business friend.

So far, the extra money I earned in modelling and acting didn't even cover the time I spent doing them. Franc was now eight and was rapidly growing out the clothes she had. And I didn't want her to have to quit her karate lessons.

This can't be my life, can it? This type of struggle was not what I had planned for my future. Running away wasn't the answer. It'd never even been a *question*. I just had to try harder.

So today after work, I was going to travel to Rosehall with Clive in a mini-bus. Rosehall didn't have good memories for me, but they could've been much worse. I knew the positive would cancel out the bad.

Clive wanted to accompany me because we were meeting his guy at a restaurant. He was going to make sure everything was above board. Even Mum was excited.

"So what kinda things yuh will have to do?" she asked.

"Clive said I'd have to meet customers, answer queries, and sometimes transport stuff into town for him," I answered.

When Clive and I got to the restaurant, the guy we were meeting was late. We sat outside in the hot evening air and waited. Clive listened to me talk about Matt Peters and my hopes for getting out as soon as I could.

Clive was quite imposing, despite his five-foot frame. His broad ex-boxer shoulders supported a head-full of long, black dreadlocks.

"Yuh still young. If I was you, I'd quit," he said, with a passion that could've been mine.

"But I can't just up and leave a paying job," I answered.

The bar and restaurant on the ground floor grew noisier by the minute. I wondered how the people in the hotel on the first floor felt about the loud voices billowing into their rest. About half an hour later when the stars began to peep out at us, Clive suggested we move inside to avoid the hungry mosquitoes.

"I gon get a drink. Wot yuh want?" he asked me when we took our seats inside the restaurant.

"Pepsi, please," I answered.

"Yuh sure? I doan mind getting you a beer, yuh know."

"Pepsi is fine," I said.

"C'mon, *one* beer won't hurt yuh. I know yuh doan drink, but tonight is for celebratin' a'int it?"

"I'm fine with Pepsi Clive, really."

He left for the bar. 'Careless Whisper' was playing on the jukebox.

Someone else must love it as much as I did. It was playing when we got off the minibus and took our seats outside – about half an hour ago. The song made me think of the last party I went to.

All the kids who hung out under Father's House knew that I loved *'Careless Whisper.'* They also knew the not-so-well-kept secret that I used to have a crush on Merrick, Aaran's uncle. He danced with me when the song played, but ignored me that night for some unknown reason.

I was sitting in my seat in the corner of the house we'd come to, looking at the hem of my only dress, when Brian appeared in the middle of the song and extended his hand to me. As we danced, he said, "What's wrong with Merrick?"

"I don't know," I said, for the first time even covertly admitting my old crush to *anyone*.

"Ah was waiting for him to come over and ask you because I know you always want to dance to this track."

"I can't believe you remembered my favourite song," I said.

"Of course! Don't let yourself get upset. Merrick's got to be crazy."

Brian didn't know how much better he made me feel. Maybe one day I should tell him. Brian and I danced through the song, and the next one.

"Ah just been on the phone . . ." Clive was handing me my bottle of Pepsi. "We'll meet him upstairs. Bring yuh drink."

Clive and I walked upstairs, carrying our drinks. He'd bought himself some kind of clear swill in a glass. The lounge upstairs was filled with old, mahogany furniture. I rested my bottle on one of the tables and began to take a seat. "No," Clive said, when I was already halfway into my chair, "We got a room over here."

I was so far into the seat by then, that it was too late *not* to sit down. I got back up, picked up my Pepsi, and followed Clive down the hall.

"Why didn't you say you had this room, Clive?"

"What?"

"How come you didn't say we were gonna be up here? Thought we were meeting him in the restaurant."

"Only *just* got the room. It's way too noisy downstairs."

"Makes sense," I answered.

There was one chair in the room, which Clive immediately moved over by the door and sat in. I sat on the bed and drank my Pepsi slowly. We chatted for a while and I started to feel out of place. *Why wasn't the man here? But surely, I could trust Clive? Why does this whole thing feel so wrong all of a sudden? Why didn't I ask more questions?*

I thought about Jerry Saunders' room and instinct told me it wasn't going to be so easy this time. For one thing, I wasn't having a period like I was then. Secondly, Jerry Saunders knew my mother, and even if he *didn't* believe my lie about having some dreadful disease, he was probably not willing to go too far.

Clive, on the other hand, might be willing to. "I need the toilet," I said. I was going to get out unbroken if the exporting man didn't show up. *Please God, Please God.*

I took a quick look around the room when I got up. There was a big mirror opposite the bed, a small wardrobe near the entrance to the washroom, a table near the foot of the bed, where I'd put down my Pepsi bottle, and the chair by the door in which Clive sat.

"Why isn't he here yet?" I sort of threw my question over my shoulder. *I was so stupid to come here. Why did I get caught in these positions and how did I not know that this was a bad idea? Why was I so naïve?*

I had a notion, which I hoped would work in my favour. Inside the washroom, I turned the tap on and rolled a thick wad of toilet paper over my hands, which I stuffed in my underpants.

"Yuh okay in there?" came Clive's voice. I could've been imagining it but was he beginning to sound a bit aggressive? I remembered him telling me about how unforgiving he was in the ring.

I looked for a lock on the door, but it was broken. It would be harder to fight him in the bathroom. I'd have to make my way out and pretend I didn't know what was up.

I've always hated movie soundtracks that made even a walk in the park feel terrifying. I was thinking of the kind of music which keeps your adrenaline pumping so freely, that you jump out of your skin even at the sight of your own shadow. I was tired of that soundtrack playing between my ears. Each time I tried to do something to better our lives, it backfired on me.

I just had to get out of this place and out of my town. I was tired of scary soundtracks and getting nowhere. No amount of adrenaline was enough to propel me to where I wanted to be, if I stayed here.

I walked back over to the bed in the darkened room. It looked like Clive had turned out one of the lights. Before sitting down, I picked up the empty Pepsi bottle and stuck my middle finger into it, as deep as it would go.

I felt like I could kill him. I knew I didn't have it in me, but the thought gave me some power to sit calmly. In the movies, I'd seen people get knocked out by a hard hit in the back of the neck. I studied my glass bottle. It was narrow around the neck and waist, and quite rounded at the hips. The bottom was solid. But even if it *was* heavy enough to knock him out, the thick dreadlocks down his neck would provide a barrier.

I'd have to break the bottle and threaten to stick it into his flesh. I'd have to make him believe I could do that.

"Why yuh holding onto dat empty bottle?" Clive asked. "Give it to me." He stretched out his hand.

Do I send out some kind of message saying, *Here! Poor girl free to abuse!* I suddenly became very angry at my life for making me so needy that I got dumped in yet another feeding trough.

In the mirror on the wall, I saw a frightened girl with sad, sad eyes. She's so panicked she's stopped speaking. She doesn't need to ask the man any questions. She knows now why he has brought her here.

Her middle finger seems stuck in the neck of the bottle, and she's rolling it from side to side on the table near the bed on which she sits. The bed is covered with a faded, cream flower-print sheet, so faded it's difficult to see what type of flowers they once were.

The short man is now sitting opposite her on his chair. He leans over to the girl, and places his hand on the girl's hand, the one to which she's attached the bottle.

The last time he asked her for the bottle the girl had said she liked holding it. She's crying, but silently. There are long tears running down her face as she thinks of a time, far away in her past when she walked through a deserted school ground on her way home from school lessons.

She recalls this time because to her it seemed like a catalyst for the rest of her life, even though she still does not understand why.

Maybe it's because this was the day she saw her guardian angel and realised that no matter how bad life was, someone behind the scenes was always there looking out for her. Maybe one day, instead of horror music, her life's soundtrack will be something else, something that includes the sound of a guardian angel who protects and takes care of her when no one else makes the time.

She realises that maybe the ingredient that comes between herself and her breakers isn't in her voice or in her eyes after all. Maybe it's the guardian angel she saw in the flesh when she was nine, the very first time he stopped them.

"Yuh shouldn't cry," the man in the mirror says to the girl, inching closer. "Yuh really stunning; really, really stunning. The first time ah see yuh, me heart skipped a beat. Yuh tall, red, and got long, beautiful hair. Ah always wanted to stroke yuh hair."

The man gets up and strokes the girl's hair while she continues to cry.

The girl is crying because she has let herself be deceived – utterly. She now knows she was so wrong in thinking that this monster was her friend when he sees her as a victim; one who would go readily into his snare because she was weak, naïve and stupid. And because she was trained to hurt in silence without defence.

The man leans in to push the girl onto the bed but she fights back. She raises the bottle-hand to strike the man on the head. The trained pugilist is too fast. He grabs the bottle, plops it out of her finger, and throws it across the room.

The girl catches sight of the man's eyes and she is sure she has *never* seen this man before. He's a stranger who's popped up in her nightmare and she knows she's not strong enough to fight him off. She finds her voice and begs, "Please, please don't do this. I'll walk away right now. I won't tell anyone. Besides, I've got my periods."

Through her lying eyes, she thinks she sees the man she knows surface for a while so she keeps begging and she's winning. She promises all kinds of forgiveness and secrecies. She promises to leave her job the next day and never say why, but she doesn't let him touch her. She finds two hands, four hands, six hands, six legs to bat away each attempt.

She sees his confusion when for a split second his hand brushes past the large wad of toilet paper she's wearing.

The man gets up after being satisfied that she is telling the truth.

"Thank you. Thank you," the girl sobs, but now she can cry out loud because she feels grateful to the man standing beside her.

"Yuh first time should be with someone yuh like," the ex-boxer, ex-soldier, ex-friend says finally, wiping his struggle-sweat off his face. And the girl wonders how he knows so much about her.

They leave the room. The girl doesn't have enough money to get home, so again she rides with the man in a mini bus. He sits close to her and she has to concentrate very hard to keep the exploding stomach acid from coming to the surface.

"Why?" was all she could build up the courage to ask in the crowded bus.

"Well, I thought that if yuh was willing to do the 'export' business, you'd be up for it."

"Why're you saying 'export' like that? Does it mean something else?"

"Don't tell me yuh doan know."

"Look at me," the girl says, turning to face him. "Do you *think* I knew?"

But he doesn't have to look at her to know the answer. Or maybe he could no longer face her.

"Okay," he says at last. "Ask anyone. It means the drug business. Yuh so stupid."

She doesn't tell him she *had* discussed it with her mum. She doesn't want him to think her mum is stupid too.

She gulps her surprise down and takes some deep breaths. Did she agree to be a drug mule without knowing it?

"Yuh got to stop being so scared of everything," is the last thing he says to her before he gets off at his stop and leaves her to get home on her own.

"I'm obviously not scared *enough*. There are a lot of scary people out there. I just didn't know I had to be scared of *you*," she tells him.

She gets home in one piece, and when her mother asks her if they met the man, she lies and says that he was held up somewhere else. Her mother is disappointed but that is better than the truth.

The next day when, after steeling herself, she turns up for work, the man in the mirror has vanished.

CHAPTER 27 – THE QUEY QUEY

The night before Solly's brother's wedding was the first time I went to a Queh Queh. I allowed myself to be swept with the lively crowd because I had no expectation of what was to come.

They'd waited until darkness fell, then left the groom's house in a pack. I followed at the rear, trying to blend with the crowd as they danced and sang traditional African songs to accompany the dynamic drumbeats through street after street.

The singing throng picked up their guests as they trawled each street. The leaders knew exactly which houses to stop at, and sang a fresh song to each new addition. We carried on, drums staying in rhythm.

When the posse got to the bride's house, I watched in fascination as a couple of the leaders lifted her out and carried her for ten minutes back to our yard.

Back at the groom's house, the celebrations started in earnest. The low, repetitive intense bass beat of the little drums proved too much for one girl, as she danced herself into a trance.

"She got comfa!" people in the crowd shouted. The only other time I'd seen someone catch comfa was when I was a little girl at Primary school. We'd had a music group in to play some African drums to our class. One little girl caught comfa so badly, she danced until she fell to the ground – and she was *still* dancing, as her body twisted and thumped to the beat. It was hours later before she came to herself.

"Why don't they stop beating the drums?" I asked someone close to me. I figured that would be the simplest thing to do to stop the trance-like state getting deeper and deeper.

"They can't do that!" she said to me.

"Why?"

"Yuh gotta beat them drums until she dance sheself out of it. If you stop now, she gonna stay in a semi-trance for a long time."

"Really?"

"Yeah. No matter how she beat sheself around and hurt sheself dancing around in she comfa, yuh can't stop the beat."

So the girl danced around in a circle under the big front house at the top of our yard, and the crowd gave her space while the drums rolled on.

The older women lead the rest of dancing under the now-cramped bottom house. I'd never learned how to do the special dance, so I stood on a stool and looked on.

"Clear out!" someone shouted after a while, and a gap appeared in the middle of the yard, leaving me a good view of the comfa girl. She seemed transformed to another world. Only the whites of her eyes were visible, and while everyone else was hitting and slapping at the mosquitoes, which had come out for their nightly feast, she was only concerned with one thing, dancing.

She was going around in increasingly wider circles with her arms stretched out at her sides. Leroy, who had catered for the entire celebration, was clapping his hands – fingers splayed – in glee. Sometimes the girl moved in perfect circles, and at other times, she seemed to jerk to one side of the yard.

When she went to her left, the crowd on that side cleared a space for her and cheered, "Whooo!" The same thing happened on the right, as the drumbeat got faster and faster. Finally, the girl's dance came in drips and dribbles, and the drummers matched her steps.

**

Everything was back to normal in our yard. The wedding was long over. The visitors were all gone and nearly forgotten, and Elaine finally left for Canada. Now the only people living in the front house were her sister-in-law, Donna and her baby daughter. There was little attraction between Des (Solly's youngest brother) and me.

I felt lost after the family had returned home. I had become very close to Solly's dad for reasons still unknown. He sat on our scrubbed, makeshift bench and talked to me, sometimes into the night.

I promised myself one night after our lengthy conversation that I would not judge any man by the standards of my father and the ones who had tried to break me, when they were so many nurturing and good men in the world; men who touched and caressed you with their kindness but *never* with their hands.

My sense of loss was made even harder because I was battling with selfishness and confusion.

The first time Dave's sisters asked my mum to go to a party with us, I didn't know if they meant it or were being kind. However, since then she's been going quite regularly with us.

I feel selfish because I know she needs the outing. However, dancing has always been an expression of freedom for *me* – it was a state in which I belonged to no one, was responsible for no one, and was happy with me and my music.

I was embarrassed when my mother came because she danced with the boys and girls I danced with. She danced to the music that was mine, and on my stage – a platform on which *I'd* finally learned to express joy.

None of my friends had to bring their mothers. I accepted it was selfish, but I felt I shouldn't have to share that part of my life with her too. This acceptance made me feel ashamed – and guilty. And the guilt turned into indignation.

When Mum danced near me, I turned the other way. And even though my love for her never waned, I realised I didn't want her there.

I was confused because after years of going to daily Mass, I was now only going on Sundays – mainly because of work. I fell asleep each night reading the rosary, but in the back of my mind I had a suspicion I was wasting my time.

If Christ thought I had so much worth that He was willing to *die* for me, I reasoned, why would He mind if I prayed directly to Him? Why, when it came to communication, would I have inexplicably lost my worth?

In a matter of weeks, I'd given up the rosary altogether. I was going to pray differently. I was going to pray to *God*.

And even when I accidentally found out that Sasha had been seeing Dave for some time behind my back, the shock wasn't enough to make me go back to the beads.

This made it clear why Aaran had stopped talking to me. After all, *I* was the one who introduced Sasha to Dave. But how could I even *guess* that my younger 'brother' would sneak into my neighbour's house when I had gone to bed?

A Guyanese Proverb: Clath easy fuh dutty, but hard fuh wash.

Translation: It's easier for a piece of cloth to get dirty than it is to clean it.

Meaning: Once your reputation is blemished, it's hard to clear your name.

CHAPTER 28 – THE BED-RIDDEN PATIENT

I now see my grandmother every day. She's finally moved to a small room in a shared house. All her life's possessions – including a mirror some long-lost friends had given us, lived there with her. I looked around her room the first time I visited and knew I didn't want to live like that when my hair turned grey.

My aunt Theresa recently had another nervous breakdown, but because there weren't enough beds in her ward, she was discharged from hospital.

I know nothing about medicine, but it was clear to me that Theresa was unwell in other ways (other than her nerves).

She didn't talk, eat, nor sleep. At 5' 10", her seventy-pound frame was light enough for me to carry.

Her bedsores and ligature marks yawned wider and wider each day because my grandmother refused to untie her from the only bed in her room.

The daily visits to my grandmother after work was not to *see* her, but to help her feed and clean Theresa.

She saved me, so I had to save *her*. I wiped her body not only with warm water I drew from the pipe in the kitchen downstairs, but with the tears that fell from seeing her once attractive body in such a mess.

I was glad she was drugged, or unconscious or *something* most times. I was glad she couldn't see the sharp bones in her hips, or how the sores were chiselling into her once black, satin flesh.

And when she was awake, she didn't know who I was. Her loud, animal groans were the only indication she knew she was still alive.

As I rubbed her back, I hoped she would never find out what I've done. She was always so protective with her purity. I shouldn't be allowed to handle her this way.

"Can I just take off the string for a bit?" I asked my grandmother while trying to feed her watery 'soup' to my aunt. I'd covered her semi-nakedness with a thread-bare half-sheet, and propped her head against a pillow. For once, her eyes were opened and slightly focused.

"She gon bite sheself," my grandmother said, but she – stripped of the power she once had over me – silently watched me untie Theresa's left hand.

"I'll leave the other one tied up," I said. I just want her to be free for a little bit." I didn't say that I wanted her to be as free as I was. She had fought for my freedom from her mother's prison. Why couldn't she enjoy hers? I wanted her to soar and touch the stars – rule the world!

"Yuh the only person who come to help me with she," my grandmother said. "You do everything so quiet without complaining. And even though me used to hurt you, yuh still come to help me."

In all my life, this was the closest my grandmother came to offering me something of an apology.

I wanted to say that I was there to help Theresa. But even *I* knew that this wasn't the whole truth. I was there for both of them.

When Theresa managed a few seconds of lucidity, she mumbled something unintelligible, like a deep-throat gargle – almost.

I was scared, pained that she might be hurting, and I really didn't want her to hurt. But she *must*. She was so ill, she must.

Two months in an uncomfortable bed, in her twenties, wearing my makeshift nappy, was not what she had in mind. I knew her best and I knew she wanted the *opposite* of this.

Her strength was only *just* enough to move her head, and sometimes her tongue seemed trapped in her mouth when she tried to move it. I didn't want her to die. But maybe dying was better for her because I could feel myself in her body, looking down at myself. *I'd* want to die!

Her life has been about serving other people – she served me. And now I was all grown. *I* get to live, so *she* should be happy; get married, have kids, have fun and satisfaction in her life – all the things she dreamed of.

I have flown free from my grandmother's prison. I have no money or nice clothes, but I go dancing with friends.

This was never the way we planned it! When we plotted our escape, it was for both of us to be free of her. I'm out there, she's in here – right bang where she started and even I, the person she protected, feel sorry for the person who's caused her so much pain. Oh, my guilt!

I wracked my brain to think of binds that were smoother than the torn strips of old clothes my grandmother used on Theresa's wrist. I didn't like the white stuff I saw in the sores there. I hoped it wasn't bone, but I shut my eyes, so they couldn't look too closely.

Theresa manages to swallow some of her 'soup,' but most of it escapes down her chin and to the side of her face. I wipe it off. I fight the gravity and liquid with the same force I fight myself.

I was a traitor because I felt sorry for my grandmother. She was stuck in a room with a sick grown-up daughter who she was told to take home and nurse until she dies.

One day on my way to work, I didn't bother to cross the road when I passed my grandmother's old house. I decided to go in and see her instead.

"So how yuh studies comin'?" she asked. Her voice was deeper than usual, and she told me she hadn't spoken to anyone in some time.

"Nearly finishing up my first year now," I answered. "We have exams soon, but I may not be able to do them."

"How come?"

"You're supposed to pay for the entire course before they let you do the exams." "Ah just got some money," she had said, almost shocking me to the ground. She genuinely never had any money. Where did she get extra money from!

"Come back tomorrow after work," she had said, "And I gon give you money for yuh exams. How much yuh want?"

I remember my old Typing school governess saying 'right place, right time and all that . . .' Goodness! How filled my life was of those.

Later, when I showed her my certificate, there was a suspicion of pleasure in her face.

But I knew she hadn't changed! If she had, she would not have tied Theresa's hands to the bed and she would have made her, *her* favourite food, instead of cooking the precious ground provision for herself and giving Theresa the water she boiled them in as 'soup.'

Each day I left my grandmother's room, I hoped that Theresa would make it through the night. I did this because I was selfish. I didn't want to have made it out and have her die with our prisoner. I wanted her life to have meant something, something more than just being *my* protector.

Yet, why did I hope she'll escape the dream state in which she exists each day. Maybe her dreams are the *very* things that save her! If she escaped them she may see the devastation of her body and lose hope.

CHAPTER 29 – THE MISSING WAGES

I remember the day Razor Da Silva invited me to meet him. It was the day after Theresa suddenly woke up after months tied to a bed. The first thing she said was, "Yuh got any food? Ah hungry."

I had been talking to Razor for a while. "Call in for a request," he had said on his show. "Call in from the villages and towns so I know you're listening."

I was surprised when *he* answered the phone instead of a technician or producer.

"Hello there, where are you calling from?" he'd said. I was taken aback because I had been calling during my lunch break for the past couple of weeks without making contact.

"I'm in New Amsterdam and I listen to your show every day at work."

"What do you like about it?"

"Your taste in music is fantastic!" I'd told him."

"You don't sound like a Berbician," he said.

"What makes you say that?"

"You're very polished. You have a good radio voice."

"Yuh sayin' people from we county can't talk good?" I asked.

"No . . . no . . ." he stuttered.

"I'm just pulling your leg."

"I deserved that!" he laughed. Then he asked me to hold on for a minute. In the background, I heard his voice on the radio, reading off a request for someone from a place I'd never heard of, and announcing the name of the track he was about to play for them.

"How do you get your show done if you spend so much time on the phone?" I asked him when he said, *Hello* for the second time.

He laughed. "I don't normally spend all this time on the phone. My technician takes most of the calls, but he had to step out."

Finally, after putting me on hold another time to speak through his microphone, Razor asked if he could call me sometime. I didn't have a phone at home, so I gave him my office number. He called me every day at lunch time for a while. By then I was accustomed to hearing the real voice at the end of the phone line, interspersed with the detached, distant one on the radio.

One day he had some news. "I'm bringing a show to New Amsterdam soon," he said. "Why don't you come along? I'll leave two tickets at the door for you and a friend. Just tell them your name."

"Really?" I was thrilled. "I haven't heard anything about that."

"We always keep a few dates and venues flexible, just in case," Razor answered.

"So our town was a just-in-case venue?"

Razor laughed again. Soon the giant posters appeared around town, and for the first time in years, Razor was bringing some of the country's best entertainers into our tiny town.

***

It was about two weeks before Razor's show. By then I'd told everyone I knew that I was going. Matt Peters said he had tickets, but when I told him I was going to *meet* Razor Da Silva, he couldn't hide the jealousy on his face. But it was more than just jealousy. His attitude bordered on hatred, as if *he* was the deserving one, and I had stolen his birthright.

He found ways to make work calls at lunchtime, when his policy had always been to take the entire hour off work – including taking phone calls.

"Yuh shouldn't talk to that Razor Da Silva," he told me. "I know his type."

That Friday, Matt Peters ran out of cash to pay me. I did the accounts, so I knew we'd had enough petty cash by the end of the morning to pay *everyone* who worked in the shop.

"Ah have to buy some spare parts and acetylene when you guys leave, so ah need the cash," he told me. "Since *you* live so close to me, I'll pay the boys and yuh can walk over to get yuh wages. Ah got some cash at the house."

I knew he was trying to spite me because 'I'd gone out and got free tickets for myself.'

"Wait until after 6 o'clock," he told me. "I'll be home slightly late."

We always had an empty food bucket on Fridays. Mum needed my wages to go food shopping on Saturday, so I desperately needed the money. Besides, I'd worked hard for it all week.

I went home and learned my lines for an upcoming play. After a scraped-together dinner, I left for Matt Peter's house, which was five minutes away.

Matt Peters regularly boasted about his fancy big house. "My three-year-old daughter got she own room!" he says.

This was quite unusual for people who lived like I do. At nearly nineteen, I was still sharing a *bed* with my Mum, let alone have my own room.

Matt Peters boasted about his assets and his achievements as though they were extensions of his private wealth of unique abilities. He behaved as if no one else had never helped him, or had anything to do with his achievements.

In his world, his abilities had originated out of *his* brain and body, which were in no way connected to any input from the rest of us, his genes, or his parents' dedication.

Matt Peters never talked about his father's old garage – the one that mysteriously vanished out of town, just before he opened his.

He opened the fancy door of his fancy house and invited me in.

"Yuh right on time," he said, "I just poured meself some liqueur."

"What's that?"

"Yuh don't know what liqueur is?"

"Clearly," I laughed to take away the annoyance I was feeling on the inside. I'd never heard of liqueur in my life! I thought he'd said 'liquor' with a strange accent. I wasn't interested in liquor *or* liqueur. I just wanted our money so we could get some food, pay the rent and survive for another week.

"It's just a very mild alcoholic drink," Matt Peters said. "I know you doan drink, so yuh will like this. It came in this nice bottle. Lemme show yuh."

Matt Peters walked to his kitchen and I followed him. He had real cupboards with doors and handles and stuff. We had an old desk to put our stove on. The desk was a present from some friends we lost to 'abroad' a long time ago.

Matt Peters held up an exotic, tall, royal blue bottle, with a long neck. There was a small amount of liqueur left at the very bottom. *Was this the bottle he kept to impress visitors with? How was he going to do his 'impressioning' once the stuff was finished?*

"Lemme pour you some, just a little bit." *Why do people try to ply me with liquor liqueur? Just leave me alone!*

"Where's your wife?"

"Oh, she with her mother. The pregnancy not going too well. She got three weeks left, yuh know."

"Yes. She told me a couple of days ago when she came into the shop," I answered. "I had no idea she wouldn't be here today."

The liquor liqueur now made sense. I started to look around for things I could feasibly pick up and hit him with if he pitched a Promoter, Side Kick, and Jerry Saunders' ball.

"Here," Matt Peters said, handing me a small glass with some greenish liquid in it. I smelled it. It smelled okay. I tasted it and found that it wasn't bad at all.

"It's nice," I told him.

"Yuh see!" Matt Peters shouted. "I told yuh. See what you missing out on?"

"I don't think I'm missing out on anything just because I don't drink. I just don't think it's something I need in my life to have fun."

"Yeah but . . ." Matt Peters said, but I wasn't finished.

"I'll drink if I choose to, but I won't make it something I *have* to have." I felt like I had made this speech a thousand times but it *still* didn't seem to make much sense to a lot of people.

"Alright, alright," Matt Peters answered. "You didn't used to be so mouthy when yuh first came to work for me. Anyway, yuh have to admit that people who drink have more fun than people who don't, though."

"Well, *you* have to admit that people who drink have more embarrassing moments, more accidents, more fights, *and* spend more money than people who don't. I suppose you have to decide which one you find easier."

"I s'pose."

"Last week I went to the Haven with a friend and he said he had a drink for me to try. He said it was called, 'screw-driver.' It was a splash of vodka in my glass of orange juice.

"Yeah, ah know. Except, *I* make it with more than a 'splash,'" Matt Peters replied, laughing.

"It wasn't too bad, but Sam had to piggy-back me all the way home."

"Is Sam your boyfriend?" Matt Peters asked.

"Not really. That was the first time we went out *together*, and it didn't last long because I felt sick after half a glass of the screwdriver thing. That's why I won't have any more of this." I put my glass down, after taking a few sips of the green drink.

Matt Peters laughed again. For the first time, I felt relaxed talking to my boss. I stood in his kitchen, still tasting his liqueur liquor on my tongue. He was standing opposite me drinking the last of his. Maybe this was what he was really like. Maybe he wasn't so bad after all, even with his womanising.

"I can show yuh even *more* fun," Matt Peters said suddenly and lurched forward. In one movement, he had wrapped his arms so tightly around me, I felt my organs would plop out of my mouth. I pushed at his hands and realised that his arms were so securely around my waist, his hands had come around the other side and were touching his own body.

"Yuh waist so small," he said.

"What are you doing? Get off me!" I shouted, beating his arms.

"Yuh can't say yuh not attracted to me. The way yuh talk and act, yuh can't say yuh don't want a man who can give yuh the high-life."

I could hear the smirk in his voice but couldn't see his face because I had closed my eyes so I won't remember his face in mine.

"What high-life?" I shouted, "A bit of green stuff at the bottom of the bottle you've been saving? I'll scream so all your neighbours will know what you are and what you do when your wife is away."

I was shaking with fear and struggling under his hold, but it did not give. I shifted my face from side to side so that he couldn't kiss me. I never wanted to feel his slimy lips anywhere near, or on me.

"Don't think ah don't know about the dictionary yuh hide in yuh desk. Don't think I don't see yuh reading it. This is what yuh been getting ready for, ain't it?"

I realised that it was hopeless to struggle. He was a big man, and I was nearly 5'11" but just 130 pounds.

"Help!" I shouted at the top of my voice. At first I thought I had broken my diaphragm but then realised that Matt Peters had let go of me so suddenly that my lungs released a rush of air.

"I guess you should leave," he said.

"My wages," I said quietly. If my mum wasn't depending on it to go food shopping in the morning, I would've left without the cash.

"See you Monday," he said as I walked out the door. Though nothing happened, I was ashamed as I stepped out into the twilight. The thought of what could've happened – yet again, made me shiver in the humid evening air.

As I walked home, I decided that I was going to hand in my notice on Monday. I couldn't work for Matt Peters any more. My Guardian angel's friends were steaming about all the overtime and time-and-a-half he was getting. I *had* to get out of being in need because this was the thing driving all the attempted attacks on me. I had to get *out* of need so I could pull Franc out of this den.

I went back home, handed Mum the wad of money for the house, just as I'd received it, and said nothing of Matt Peter's attempt. Mum was feeling a bit under the weather, and I didn't want to make her worry. On Monday, I furiously worked through my panic on my walk to work. I handed in my two-weeks' notice. Tuesday, my dictionary was gone and so was I on Wednesday.

He didn't sue me.

CHAPTER 30 – THE GARDEN CITY

When I told Dave that I'd left my job, he suggested I visit Georgetown with him and Sasha. They had planned to go to the city for the massive annual Folk Festival, and were going to stay with his cousin for two nights.

Throwing caution to the *wind* or to anywhere else scared me, but I agreed. I felt I had nothing to lose.

When I met Razor on his show in our town, he had pecked me on the cheek and asked if he could buy me a drink. I had asked for an orange juice and was brought (by various waiters) bottles of orange juice throughout the night. No one brought me liquor liqueur, rum, bubbly or anything else. I had enough juice to keep Sash and me hurrying to the *Ladies* all night.

Before I left he had said, "If you ever come to Georgetown and need a friend to show you around, let me know." I didn't think he was serious, but it was nice to know I had the option.

I thought that all the recent events were pointing me to the Capital city to find the help my family so desperately needed. *I* had to be the one to break to the surface or we'd live under the hard shell of poverty for the rest of our lives.

I filled two tattered, second-hand sports bags with everything I owned. I planned to return after the festival, so packing all my belongings was a bit redundant. I had ten dollars, not even enough to buy my lunch, let alone pay my mini-bus fare. Dave and Sasha would pay my passage, and if I didn't come back with them, I'd be stranded. I said goodbye to Mum and Franc and promised to see them soon.

Dave's cousin was taking us out for a look-around the city and then we were going dancing. We crashed in one bedroom, all over the floor and the bed. I couldn't *wait* to go out into the streets and when we did, my child-like delight was hard to contain.

For so many years, I had heard the names of the City's streets on the radio. I had heard of the shops in adverts and had seen the pictures of the front of some of them in the papers.

It was hard to believe I was *actually* looking at them. I had crawled into the little radio on the ledge in our tiny room, and was walking around inside it – at least that's what it *felt* like.

This was radio world. It shouldn't be real but I could touch the wood and stone! Later, after a night of dancing, I told Dave's cousin that I had had an invitation to see Razor Da Silva, so he promised to take me to the radio station the next day.

Sleep didn't find me that night. I had no plans. I didn't know what I was going to do, or where I was going to live – live? Live? Why was I thinking about living? I was here for a couple of days. That was all!

But by the end of the night, it was clear why I'd packed *all* my worldly possessions without thinking about it. I wasn't going back to New Amsterdam. Suddenly, I'd made the decision that I was going to stay. I didn't know where or how.

I'd come this far. I wasn't going back to be meat for the butchers in my town. My sister had to have a better life so she wouldn't fall into their trap. I realised I may have been the *only* girl at which they stopped short. I was acutely aware that my sister and mum needed food. I would look for a job on Tuesday, but this holiday Monday, I would be normal for just *one* day.

"You look fabulous!" was the first thing Razor said to me.

"Thank you," I answered. I'd been waiting for about half an hour because he was still on air when I arrived. The radio in Reception was tuned to his station and when he got the message that I was waiting, he said hello to me – on air. My life was becoming more surreal by the minutes that ticked past.

"I've taken you up on your invitation and here I am. I've got the rest of the afternoon," I said to him.

I expected Razor to be taken aback. I'd turned up without warning on a holiday Monday. What was I thinking!

"You've got perfect timing!" he said. "I'm doing an emcee shift at the Festival and am just heading to the park. My taxi's outside." Razor offered his arm and I took it.

Now I could see him in the light of day, Razor was as tall as me. Solly had about twenty pounds on him, but not much more than that. He was clearly older than me, but I couldn't guess by how much.

"So, have you ever been to a folk festival?" Razor asked.

"Never been to the city apart from once, when I was a little girl. I hear about the festival on the radio all the time, though."

"You will love it. It's one of my biggest promotions every year."

"So how come you're here, and not there?" I asked.

"I decided years ago that I couldn't do an entire day of hosting on my own. I just go down there for the afternoon, especially if I'm doing my radio show too."

The chauffeur seemed to know Razor well, and when we got to the park, people at every corner called out his name. Many came over to the open window of the car and high-fived him or shook his hand. The car was moving about five miles an hour by then, dredging a path between the sea of people.

The sun, even though it was about two in the afternoon, seemed right overhead. I was boiling hot in the back seat with the windows down, and "Shaggy" was blaring from speakers in the park.

Every ten minutes or so, Razor turned around, took my hand and asked me if I was okay. I felt slightly uncomfortable, as I'd never had my hands held – not like that.

When I was a little girl, the only person who held my hand was my aunt Theresa, and she always grabbed my wrist. She said my sweaty palms made her hands clammy. But Razor didn't seem to mind.

"Can we pull over?" Razor asked his driver. "I think we can walk faster than this."

The driver laughed. "At least yuh got protection from the sun in here," he replied, but he stopped the car.

"Yuh driving tomorrow or ah picking yuh up?" he asked as Razor paid him.

"I'll drive my car. Got some business to do in town in the morning."

On foot, Razor and I came to a patch of grass where a group was having a picnic next to their tent.

"People camp out here?" I asked.

"Yeah. Every year we've had more and more campers. Saves the trouble of driving into the park today."

As we passed them, the crowd called out to Razor by name. A few of them got up and came over to ask for photos.

The attention scared me, especially after some of them insisted that I joined in. How could *anyone* stand all this devotion all the time!

Razor waved at them and we continued to walk through the blanket of people in the park. Many stopped to shake Razor's hand or to pat him on the back. He laughed with them as if he knew them well.

We approached a food stand with a healthy barbecue already going. "Razor!" the chef called out, "Anything on the house, mon?"

"Wat yuh got?" Razor asked, taking my hand and walking over. In an instant he'd switched from his radio accent to one I had not heard him use before.

"Raze, my man!" the cook took his hand and pumped it like a barbell. I got bread, barbequed chicken, cheese rolls, black pudding, souse, you name it, I got it. And for yuh lady as well. All on Billy from Campbelville, mon."

"What yuh want?" Razor turned to me to ask.

"Just chicken, please," I said quietly, "And a drink." I felt a pang of guilt each time someone bought or offered me something that wasn't mine to have.

"Chicken and orange juice for the lady, please, and the same for me, bro," Razor said.

We continued to walk to the hub of the festival, from where Razor would be doing his emceeing.

"Why didn't you say I wasn't your lady?" I asked. "You're giving your friend the wrong impression.

"Well, I don't know the guy," Razor answered, going back to the way he spoke on the radio. "And secondly, no guy is going to correct anyone who *thinks* you're his lady – not when you're so beautiful."

I laughed, but on the inside I was still battling years' old taunts of being too ugly to be loved, having a neck that resembled that of a scavenger bird, and being too skinny to be pretty. I was re-grooming myself – making *me* believe that I looked on the outside, the way I was trying to feel on the inside – beautiful.

"I can't get over the fact that everyone knows you," I said, changing the subject. "How on earth do you deal with all this attention?"

Razor laughed. His laughter was deep and rich.

"They know that I'm for the everyday man. See the guy with that barbecue stand."

"Uh huh."

"He knows that tomorrow I'll talk about his food on my radio show. He knows he can *count* on that. On Wednesday, he will run out of food. By the end of the month, he has to get rid of his road stall and rent a shop."

"The radio station *let* you do that?"

"Well . . ." Razor paused in thought. "Not exactly. But see, they pay me to talk. Who's gonna say I can't talk about my experience with Billy from Campbelville and his exquisite chicken? Man, this is good!"

"Free advertisement?"

"Exactly."

"I bet the big businesses you advertise for don't like that."

"Guess not. They pay thousands for one minute of some jingle, and Billy from Campbelville gets an honest review free. I grew up in poverty, Anne. I've *never* forgotten what an empty belly feels like. I said I don't know the people who shook my hand, but I probably do. Maybe years ago, I ran them out of a road-side stall or a front-yard car shop."

Razor laughed again, but I was deep in thought.

We finished our chicken in silence, but it wasn't uncomfortable. I didn't expect it to be.

"So where're you staying?" Razor asked finally.

"At my friend's cousin. But I have to leave in the morning when they go back home."

"Where're you going next?"

"Haven't worked it out yet. I just decided I might *actually* stay in the city."

"Wow, I misjudged you!"

"How so?"

"That's a bold thing to do. Just up and leave home without a plan. I like that."

"You're joking, right?" I asked. "That's the most foolish decision I've ever made – and I've made some *idiotic* ones."

"Let me know if I can help. Anything."

"Maybe I'll try calling my uncle. I'm not sure." I didn't know I *was* going to call my estranged uncle until I said so.

"He lives in the city?"

"Yeah," I answered. "Uncle Daniel doesn't really speak to the family. He's a rich magistrate. Kinda looks down his nose at us. He sort of *escaped* the family a long time ago."

"You think it's a good idea to call him?"

"Yep."

The finality in my answer surprised me. Clearly, I was turning into someone else. I didn't know how to *be* someone else. I liked this person I knew. I knew what this person was going to do next. I knew how this person felt and I could depend on this person to be good.

My fear was that the person I was turning into may not *want* to be good – couldn't be *trusted* to be good. Or maybe I was just scared of the mass of people, some of whom were half dressed because of the intense heat burning down on their bodies. I had never seen this many people all together in my entire life. Was my life really so insulated?

Maybe I didn't know if I could trust the man next to me. I glanced at him; his jet-black hair clung to his forehead and the sun seemed to have no darkening effect on him.

"If you run into trouble you could always stay at my house. I'm almost never there. Lisa, my daughter, visits whenever she wants, but apart from that, my house is usually empty." "Where's Lisa's mother?" I asked.

"She doesn't live far away at all. We weren't married – just had a child together. That's all we share, really."

"How old is she?"

"Who, my daughter's mother?"

"No, Lisa."

"Twelve. And she is becoming very jealous of me, but there is nothing to worry about. I'll tell her who you are."

"I think I'll call my uncle."

"Okay. I'll take you back to the radio station after we leave here. We could call him from there. That okay?"

"Yes, thank you."

"I'll get my guy to take you back to your friends tonight. Anything else I can do?"

"No. You're really kind."

"I got one condition."

"What's that?"

"That you relax and enjoy today."

"Okay," I told him, but I was panicking about what my uncle would do when I turned up in his life. This was a man who didn't speak to my mother – a man who visited us *once* in the last twelve years, only because he was ruling in a case near to where we lived. I could only wait and see.

CHAPTER 31 – THE VALUE OF A TATTERED BAG

"My family, my family!" Uncle Daniel said, shaking his head distastefully from side to side. The action took him little energy, but it elbowed me off the 'beautiful' ladder I was trying to climb internally, and slammed me face down to wallow in the dust like the flea I was.

Razor had picked me up from Dave's cousin the morning after the festival. He brought me to the radio station, where my uncle had agreed to pick me up.

"What a disgrace!" he continued, as yet again he weighed my blue, tattered bag in his hand. We had just walked away from saying goodbye to Razor, me carrying one of my bags, and he, the other. I wondered if Razor was even out of earshot.

"People know who I am in this town. I shouldn't be holding a bag like this."

I wanted to say that the stranger we'd just left had carried the bag without noticing its worth; that for him, an old bag did not make him less of a person. But I kept silent.

"A big magistrate like me . . . this is why I can't take my family."

After a couple of minutes, we got to where Uncle Daniel had parked his car. I didn't know how long I was going to stay with him and his family, but it would probably be until I found a job.

"I'm really impressed with your car," I told him. "It's so clean and tidy. Smells of fresh oranges."

"Thank you," he said.

I'd headed to the back seat when he opened the doors. I thought that maybe I, the scruffy-bag woman wasn't allowed up front, but Uncle Daniel gave me a look that told me I was to sit next to him.

I was impressed that he could drive. I gazed at the buttons in his car, suppressing a sudden urge to press them. One of them lit up as if to say, *Come on, do it. You know you want to.*

I lay my head against the back of the seat and tried to enjoy the cool air that had followed the sudden downpour, fifteen minutes before Uncle Daniel arrived. The rain had come like an enormous wave – as if a whale had splashed the contents of the Atlantic onto the Demerara shore.

It came with a roar, with fat, white drops of water pelting down noisily on the roof and on the ground. It rained hard as usual and so thick, it created a white net curtain of wet. Then it was over ten minutes later. It was gone just as suddenly as it had come.

The sun was out again, and apart from the wet ground, there was no sign it had rained.

Back at his house, Uncle Daniel introduced me to his wife and two sons, Adam 4, and Kieran 6.

"Kate is in Barbados on holiday," he said, stressing *Barbados*. It was as if he knew with certainty that Barbados was way out of my reach, out of my plane of existence. Instantly, I thought of his mother (my grandmother) and how she scrubs every cent of every dollar to *barely* get by.

She had to depend on us, who weren't much better off, for food. I couldn't also help sparing a thought for my mother, his sister who had nothing more than what *her* teenage daughter could give her, while her brother's teenage daughter spent her school holiday in Barbados.

Yet, I felt encouraged by his life and his ability to send his kids on holiday, something I thought only foreigners did.

If *he* could make it out of poverty, so could we! We too could have three bedrooms in our house. We too could have a large garden and even a gas cooker one day! *But we mustn't forget where we came from. And we mustn't forget the people who're still there.*

Uncle Daniel had been a lawyer for some time before becoming a magistrate. He'd worked hard for his status in life. If I worked hard too, I could build something better for us.

I woke up before the family each day. I was going to prove my worth to them, taking nothing more than was *absolutely* necessary. I was going to give as much as I could, to leave them richer than they were when I arrived.

By my third day with them, I had a feeling their wealth had suffocated their prosperity in happiness and smiles.

In the awkward silence of their home, everyone moved about doing precisely what they had to do. My aunt spoke only when necessary, and then, extremely quietly.

Within three days, I'd written fifty job application letters by hand. I addressed the envelopes carefully and licked them shut with a numb tongue. Once I'd finished all the housework, I surprised the family by cooking dinner, something I wasn't very good at doing as yet.

None of my attempts at embracing the family got my uncle's attention. If they did, he never mentioned it.

The only thing he extended were accusations – and *they* were thrown. To him, I knew nothing and that was the way I would remain. There was no scope, no chance of me learning anything more than what I knew at *that* moment.

He taunted me about my choice of paper. "You people know nothing. Is this the paper you want to use to send out applications? I wouldn't read *anything* sent to me on this paper," he said, thumbing through my unfinished applications. I held my breath as I stood next to him, hoping that he didn't read one of them and find a spelling mistake.

I stood transported to ten years old, when my daily tormentor grilled me like a police officer. I was too scared to say that I used the cheaper paper because I didn't want to touch his nicer writing pads.

"How many letters have you written today?" He asked each day.

It stung my flesh that I had to ask him for money to buy stamps to post the letters, day after day. And when he arrived home each afternoon, I almost vomited with stress when he threw the money down on the desk in front of me.

It pained me to eat his food in the silence around their table, the soft chewing making me feel I had to eat as little as possible. The family acceptance I yearned for was pitifully absent.

Did I invade their house? They looked uncomfortable. Did I make them uncomfortable? My sharpened tension antennas indicated all sorts of currents – and none of them good.

The only question was how long my skin could bear the repulsive volts of the big, rich, unhappy house. I was beginning to feel like my old self – the old scared little girl I was. I was transformed to the child whose stomach was such a tight ball of nerves, she couldn't keep any food down. When did I get back here? I thought I was growing stronger.

I was nearly nineteen, but my upbringing had left me wired in such a way that fuses sparked and shorted at an alarming rate in my frail body.

My aunt walked the perfect tightrope of speaking to me only when necessary without being unkind.

Was I in her way? If she wasn't impressed by all the housework I did, I would tackle their garden as well, where the grass in the back was a foot tall. This would surely break their reserve and allow me to seep into their iron bars.

I found an old, rusty cutlass (machete) they kept in the storeroom downstairs, and chopped the grass, handful by handful, just as I'd seen the cane cutters do it.

Day after day, after I wrote more application letters, and guiltily licked the stamps, I went out into the blazing sun and hand-cut their grass inch by inch. I was going to change my aunt and uncle's minds about me. I was going to show them *my* hand of friendship and earn their trust, even if I had to break my back doing it.

When neither the housework nor the extreme gardening worked, I decided that maybe the thing they needed help with most was the boys. I had a good reading voice, so I would use it to read to and entertain them.

I resolved that the only thing I would take from them was their food, the paper I used to write my applications, and their stamps. I was going to give back as much as I could, especially since the stuff I used seemed so important to them.

I determined to make one more attempt to find the human who used to live where my uncle now existed. Tomorrow, I planned; tomorrow I would tackle the pasture in front of the house.

I knew the grass would take all day to cut, so as soon as Uncle left to do his 'magistrating' the next morning, I prepared for my big surprise.

I'd been putting off the hardest task for some time because my back ached from hours of bending over, both my hands were badly calloused from days of cutlass-weeding, but more so because the front grass was knee-high and had nettles and insects nesting among them.

Within the first five minutes of chopping grass, I was stung from face to toe. Angry, red spots flared on my skin, dark from the previous days' burns, but I had a high pain threshold.

A few of my old blisters had finally burst against the many hundreds – no, many *thousands* of chop-chop friction from the wooden and iron cutlass handle. I used one of my old tee-shirts to tie up my hands and continued. I'd started, so I was going to finish. An unfinished job doesn't make a *great* surprise.

CHAPTER 32 – THE DOG POT

"Jobs are a scare commodity these days," Razor said.

"I really *have* to find one soon. I have no way of knowing what's going on at home without writing a letter, and that takes ages to get there and back."

"What, you want your mum to read your letter, and send it back?" Razor smiled.

"You know what I mean. I'm serious. Don't try to make me laugh."

"Don't worry, Stretch."

"Stretch?" I smiled at his name for me. It was better than, *That one*. "I spent all those hours yesterday telling you my situation. Clearly, I've *got* to worry."

"You've had *years* of working hard. Take a few months off on me. I got a fabulous tour in Essequibo in two weeks. Come, have fun. I'll send some money for your Mum and sister."

"You can't do that . . ." I started.

"Why do you find it so hard to take stuff? Learn to live. Relax. In my line of work, everyone does favours for everyone else. Please, say you'll come."

"I've never been to Essequibo . . ."

"You've never been *anywhere*," Razor laughed, and he was right.

Essequibo was the unexplored county I only *heard* about on the radio. It was a place whose beauty I could only imagine. I'd heard about its rain forests, its jungles and water falls; about its streams and rivers that flowed as clear as tears and as black as night.

I'd heard of its richness in gold and diamond, of its giant five-hundred-year old turtles, and of its aboriginal people; wealthy in their culture and indigenousness.

"The crew and the back-up artists will go on the ferry but I've got a speed boat booked." Razor was saying.

"I didn't say I was going."

"I know you will," he said. He seemed to know everything about me, in the short space of time we'd talked. He knew what I was about to do next, and had answers to the questions even I didn't know I was about to ask. I knew that if I went with him, I'd have to be with him. Could I do that?

"Okay," I answered, after some time.

I was shocked that there was so much *life* and living out there in the real world, so much I didn't even *think* existed. I spent three weeks with singers, dancers, musicians and magicians.

Razor's entertainers invaded hotel after hotel, show after show, town after town; setting off neon, sizzling flames, leaving the locals panting and clawing for more. Backstage, alcohol was consumed in gallons, cigarettes were lit by the thousands, and pounds of marijuana were inhaled.

The first time I refused the drug I was called, "Country Girl" and "Impostor." By the end of the first week, my insistence of abstinence was merely laughed at – that was until Razor found out.

As promoter and host, he was top stage and didn't see what was going on in the wings. Though he *never* used drugs, he didn't tell his performers not to. When he found that my refusal of drugs, cigarettes and booze backstage was met with scorn, he went wild, vowing to leave the groups and individuals out of his next gig.

"She will be the way she *wants* to be!" he said to them, with a fierceness I hadn't seen in him before. "Keep her out of your mess!"

We all got along better after that.

Back to Razor's house, I was shocked to see how he lived the first time I visited with my raw hands.

"The few pieces of furniture I have include two beds and a couch," he told me, before we walked in.

"No cooker?" I asked, once I'd walked around the kitchen.

"No cooker," he replied. "I always eat at work."

"You couldn't tell from the outside of the house," I said.

Razor lived in one of the most elite parts of the city. Unlike Leroy, Miss Bessy, and the other characters in my street back home, Razor was neighbour to Ambassadors, famous businessmen, politicians and writers, foreign landowners and hoteliers.

"Rita did it," he said, as if that summed up the answers to all the questions I had in my head.

"Who's Rita?"

"She lived with me. We had a good life, the most beautiful home, and have a seven-year-old son together. Five years ago, I went abroad for a gig, and when I came back, my house was empty.

"You've lived like this for *five* years?"

"Yep. She left nothing; no plates, pots, TV, radio, nothing. She even took our dog, the cutlery, the curtains. The worst thing . . ." Razor cleared his throat. "The worst thing, well, apart from taking my son, she took my gold watch that *I* won in a 'Best D.J' contest. That was mine, not *ours*."

"Sorry about that. Is that why you're out so much?"

"Yes. I live here, but I don't live here, if you see what I mean. My maid comes twice a week, and Lisa – whenever she wants."

I knew exactly what he meant. My uncle had a huge house and a comfortable settee, which I'd never seen him relax on. I wracked my brain to remember if I'd *ever* seen him relax.

"Sometimes I pay Lisa's mum to cook for me," Razor continued, "But most times I eat at work or out. Not good for my figure I must say," Razor pointed to his round belly.

"Why did Rita do that to you?" I asked. "I mean, it feels like she was punishing you for something."

"I was seeing someone else."

"Oh," I said, not surprised. I'd seen the way women behaved when he was around.

Two days later, I had set up a fire-side in the back garden just beyond the cherry tree where none of the high-flying neighbours could see it. I figured that if they saw the smoke, they would think it was from a barbecue.

I'd found a few bricks around the large garden, which I set up side by side on top of each other. I thought that if I cooked a meal, the first in the house for five years, it would be a start of a new life for Razor.

After all, no one deserved to live like he did. I wanted to help him, to make his life better – to save him.

"I found a pot," I told him when he came home from work. I'd started to write some jingles for him and was in the process of cleaning out one of the three bedrooms, which was chocked full of records and tapes. I thought Jerry Saunders' twenty cassettes were impressive. Well, Razor had more than a hundred times more!

"Where?" Razor asked.

"In the kennel."

"Oh, the dog used to eat in that!" he cried.

"I scrubbed it up."

"Yeah?" Razor laughed.

"Yeah, and I went to the corner shop."

"They don't have much more than stale cigarettes in there," Razor answered.

"They had paper plates and enough for me to cook you a meal in the pot I found. We'll have to eat with the tea spoons though, because . . ."

"You cooked me a meal?" Razor looked incredibly surprised but almost immediately, he began to weep.

"You cooked me a meal," he cried, over and over. "In the dog pot."

I couldn't understand why he was so moved because of one little meal. We'd gone out and sent money for my Mum and sister, and spent a lot getting me new clothes for our trip. (The first thing I picked out was a pair of jeans. I'd always wanted some). He'd done *more* for me than cook a meal.

"Yeah I had to empty the rice in some of the plates, then cook the stew after."

"What did you cook on?" Razor was still crying, but there was a sort of happy incredulous look on his face too.

"I made a fire-side."

"I thought you were allergic to smoke."

"I am."

"How . . .?" he began to cry again, but I didn't want to have to re-light the smoky fireside. Doing it *once* was too much. I took his hand and said, "Let's eat."

We ate by candle light because of the black-out; eating from our paper plates piled with rice and stewed chicken. We steadied our plates on a tiny, old coffee table I'd rescued from the back of his second bedroom, which was overflowing with suits he'd worn once on shows, then no more.

Hundreds of pairs of shoes of different colours, lay forgotten in the dust of the 'clothes' room.

"You brought me my life back," Razor said. "And you brought it with a dog pot I'd forgotten I had. I'm never letting you go now."

The dog pot seemed to have a deeper meaning to Razor, one that I could never understand fully.

"Well, we need to buy some kitchen stuff tomorrow," I told him later, wheezing heavily. "I can't cook on the fireside again, and I also don't think it's fair – and awkward – to ask Lisa's mother to cook for me."

One of the musicians Razor knew had my last name. It took him a few minutes to discover that the guitarist was my first cousin, who I'd never met.

This action rolled like a large snowball in an avalanche, resulting in me meeting hundreds of my dad's relatives, all of whom I had never met – and didn't know about. Within hours, my cousin led us to his dad, Compton, my father's older brother who lived about an hour outside the city.

Once Razor had driven me to his house and Uncle Compton had instantly swept me up into his arms (even before I had a chance to decide whether his grass needed cutlassing or not), he pointed to the house next door and said, "Let's go see yuh dad and yuh sisters. Horace!" he called out, throwing his voice upstairs. "Come see your sister!"

My dad had finally retired from old job, and had moved in with Uncle Compton's landlady. So had Sue and another sister, who were both working in the city. Horace, one of my brothers, was living with Uncle Compton, his partner, her sons, and a couple of other relatives.

Why didn't I think of my father's family when I thought of the city? This of course, was where they all lived!

Right-place-right-time and Razor found my family just after my ninety-year-old grandmother had returned from Canada to live in her adopted home, Guyana. She lived with her daughter, my aunt Babs, which gave us another trip to make, to a house I'd never visited, to an aunt, cousins (and grandmother) I'd never seen.

Hundreds of strangers – of family who knew how to breed, were embracing me like they'd known me forever, especially my Uncle Compton and his partner, Aunt B. My grandmother's sweetness was more pronounced by how different she was from the other one I used to call *Mammy*.

Overnight, my life was extended by people who shared my genes.

And so began my first year in the big city. I missed many things from home. Most of all, I missed my autonomy. I missed the freedom of going out for walks in our small town, and seeing my friends.

It occurred to me, especially towards the end of the first year that I had lost myself. I wrote, cooked and did the washing and cleaning on the days the maid wasn't due in. At nights, I got dressed up to mix with the city's elite.

I couldn't see it at first, but slowly everything was about Razor, even the writing work I did was in support of his job. We went to *his* gigs and his parties. We saw *his* friends.

"You don't need to wait for me at the market," I said to Razor one day. "I can go on my own and you can pick me up when I'm done."

"It's okay," he answered. "I really don't mind."

But *I* minded. I wanted at least *some* independence. I'd failed to see his possessiveness in the early days. I guess because my experience in those things was painfully lacking.

Last food shopping day, as Razor dropped me off, I took a glance at a brand new sports car I saw in the street. A year ago, I'd made it my business to be able to tell the make and model of *any* car without having to look at the insignia. At first it was part of my job, then it became a personal challenge.

I'd never seen this type of car before, but Razor saw my glance and assumed I was looking at the driver. He didn't speak to me for four days.

"You know I get angry even if you look at a frog," was his apology, but the silent treatment had become routine to our lives.

"You know this attitude takes the joy out of every new experience I have, and the thrill of every new and fascinating person I meet – people and experiences you sometimes go out of your way to expose me to," I answered.

"I just can't help it. I don't want anyone to steal you away from me."

"That's just silly, though. No one can get *stolen*. People leave. Do you know that I've resorted to being rude to every man who speaks to me? That's not me and it feels really bad. I can't have any fun. I go around with a frown on my face so men in the crowd or at our table don't speak to me. I try *not* to be noticed and that's not fair."

"Well, it's not fair on *me*. I have to look for you when I'm on stage to make sure no one's talking to you," was his reply.

Razor just didn't get it. I prayed on every occasion we went out that no one spoke to me but they did, and the experience which should've been new, happy and enjoyable, turns out to be agonising.

It took me back to a time when my grandmother beat me any time she saw – not me talking to a boy, but any boy talking to *me*.

I have good relationships with new-found cousins, aunts and uncles, and I see Mum and Franc often. It fills me with content when I can send for them on school holidays, because they get to do something I've never done, go on vacation – even if it's only to the city.

They're never in need of anything, but I know that someday I'll have to do something that might change their lives significantly. I know I'll have to leave Razor for my own sanity. Whatever I wanted, this wasn't it.

CHAPTER 33 – BARBADOS

This is why when my English pen friend of two years, Hilary, wanted to meet in Barbados, his birthplace, I agreed.

He would send me a return ticket. We would stay at his mother's house for three weeks, and I'd see Barbados. It was a struggle to convince Razor to let me go.

It was Hilary's name that first gave me the cunning idea. I lied to Razor, saying that he was my long lost friend from school, a *girl* called Hilary, who wanted to see me again (I did have a long-lost friend from school who happened to be living in Hilary's city).

Hilary – a doctor – and I had nothing at all romantic. We were merely friends, but I knew Razor would never believe that.

After much effort on my part, he surprisingly agreed that I could go, providing I gave him all of Hilary's particulars and phone numbers. I did, but they were all made-up.

It was the first time I had flown on a plane and I was slightly nervous. Hilary had sent me ten pounds sterling for extra expenses and this was all the only money I had on me.

I felt a fool for coming all this way to a strange country where I had no one and didn't know what was about to happen. *How is it that I only see the clear signs of a mistake after making it?*

It didn't help that the customs officers pulled me over to check my bags. They removed each piece of clothing in detail, looked in the bottom of my bags, felt under the lining, and examined the pockets. I was surprised when they asked for the number of the lady I was staying with, and made a phone call to her. Whatever Hilary's mother said was convincing enough, because after half an hour of private questioning, I was allowed to go.

They dumped my carefully folded clothes back into the bags and threw my papers in for good measure.

I instantly recognised Hilary when I saw him from a distance, waiting in the empty airport foyer. He seemed much shorter than his pictures indicated.

The surprised look on his face bothered me, but maybe I wasn't what he was expecting. After all, he'd only ever seen *one* grainy picture of me.

"You are so much more beautiful than your picture!" he said, before saying hello. By then I'd walked up to him and asked if he was Hilary.

"You *are* expecting me, right?" I asked heart in my mouth. He still seemed unsure.

"Yes, yes, sorry," Hilary replied. He introduced me to the man standing behind him as his brother. Finally, once we had my bags in his brother's car, I exhaled a thousand breaths.

His brother dropped us off at a cottage, which looked like a self-catering holiday home. "You said we were staying with your mum's," I said quickly, already sensing that I had made a big mistake.

"Yes, I'm afraid I changed my mind," Hilary said, in an accent very much like the ones I heard on B.B.C radio back home. "My mother isn't very well at the moment and she can't entertain."

I didn't quite believe him, but I should've had no doubts. Solly's dad and Hilary on one side of the scale, were enough to weigh down the breakers all stacked up on the other.

After we'd had a late night dinner, Hilary said we had to talk.

From across the table at the restaurant, I could see he was as nervous as I felt, maybe just as scared too.

"Okay," he began, "Let me finish before you say anything. I may not have made it clear in my letters." I silently hoped this was not another Rose Hall episode because this time I had no home to go to.

"I really *am* attracted to you and I thought that we could be a couple. I could take you to live with me London. All you have to do is say yes. I've had no time to date and find someone. I want to marry and have kids. I'm older now and I don't really fancy British women. You pour your soul out in your letters. You're an open book, and that's what I love about you."

"But we spent the last year talking about Razor and me," I told him. "And that I was thinking of *how* to leave. You know I'm not in the right frame of mind for any of this right now."

"I know. That's why I sent for you. Like I said to you, you needed a break from him to really make the decision."

"I feel so bad. It's occurring to me *just* how naïve I am! When you invited me to Barbados, it was only for us to meet. You never said anything else. I knew you were a good person, so when you said come, I thought it was because of the things I'd said about Barbados – even *before* I knew you were born here – and how much I wanted to see the place."

"That was part of it too. After all, Mum lives here and I visit every year. Why *wouldn't* I want you to come and visit? We're friends, right?"

"That's exactly what I thought!"

"Look, Anne. I work hard to make a name for myself in England. I invest time in the friendship we've had for two years, and in the letters I write to you. I know that you have to wait until you go to your mum's house to get them, so I put a lot into them, as if I were wrapping a present for you each time. Why are your eyes closed, Anne?"

"I have to leave tomorrow."

"What, go back home?" Hilary asked.

"Yes. I got everything wrong, I'm closing my eyes because I feel so bad and I can't look at you."

"Please open them."

"I can't. I have to keep them shut," I replied.

"So you'll keep them closed while I talk to you?"

"Yes. It makes this easier."

"I really do like you. And now that I've actually seen you, I can see why you don't fancy me. I'm older, balding . . ."

"It's not that. You'd believe me, if you saw the man in the relationship I am getting out of," I said.

"So I'm right. You don't fancy me?"

"No. I'm sorry. I didn't think we were doing the fancying thing. I came because you said we were staying with your mother. Remember that conversation we had? You were going to stay in *your* bedroom, and I could have your sister's old one?"

"I can take you to the travel agent tomorrow."

"Okay."

We walked back to the cottage in awkward silence. We agreed that until I got a flight back, he would spend time with his mum, and I would hang around and visit the nearby beaches. As soon as I left, he would spend the rest of his holiday in his mother's house. We hoped I could get a flight in a couple of days.

When we got back, Hillary opened the front pocket of his bag and said, "Here Anne. I brought you something."

"You still want to give it to me?"

"Yes, of course! I got you some Poison. I asked the ladies at work for recommendations. They said it smells very nice."

"Thank you."

"Put it on."

"Okay. Sorry this is all so awkward," I said again.

"Yeah, um . . ."

"Where will I sleep tonight?" I asked. This was the first question on my mind when I walked into the cottage and saw one double bed in the bedroom.

"The bed is actually two singles," Hilary replied uncomfortably. I thought . . . you know . . . just in case. We can pull them apart to opposite ends of the room."

"Okay. I've got you a present too. It's just a small piece of Guyanese Amerindian craft." I went to unpack his present, after helping Hilary separate the beds.

The next morning we went to the travel agent. The first flight to Guyana was in nine days' time. Hilary and I agreed that we were going to divide the cleaning and cooking.

Since all I had was the ten pounds he'd sent me, the only thing I could do was to spend my days across the road at the wide white beach and go for walks. This is exactly what I did.

CHAPTER 34 – THE GOOD LISTENER

"So are you saying he is not what you want from a boyfriend?"

"No, not really," I answered. "He wants me to want the things *he* wants me to want. Know what I mean?" I looked over to Andy and he was nodding his head and smiling.

I have more shoes and clothes than I can wear, but I want respect and happiness. I want a pure and simple life."

"Material things are not enough."

"Exactly."

Right-place-right-time or was it guardian-angel-overtime-duty? Andy had saved my life the first afternoon I wandered out to the beach. I'd spent the morning at the travel agent, at the supermarket, then finally back at the cottage to cook lunch for Hilary and me. The rest of the afternoon was mine – until dinnertime that was. Hilary was spending the afternoon at a cricket match with his brother.

The clear, blue water was invitingly warm. I'd seen pictures of Barbados for years, never imagining I would feel the soft, white sand of its shores between my toes. I was as alone as anyone could be, in a place I didn't know, but I wasn't lonely. I was excited, happier than I'd been in years!

I'd never learned to swim. The closest I got to water, was paddling in a ditch with Sue and my other brothers and sisters in their village. Back then, it was Sue who had saved me from drowning when she pulled me from the bottom of the muddy trench.

The Bajan water was absolutely clear, so clear, that as I stood up in the water, I could see the floral design on my black swim-suit. The waves were monstrous, though. And when they came in, the beach was so welcoming, they stayed put. This is what got me into trouble. I thought that I was paddling in a safe place, right where the water came up to my waist.

When the tall wave came in and covered me, I had just enough breath left to fight until it went back out, that is, *if* it went back out.

The shock left me dumbstruck. I was too panicked to call out for help, and as I went below the water a third time, I felt strong hands pull me up from behind.

Those hands were Andy's. Since then, we've met each day on the beach, in the same spot – all without planning. Andy was on his own, and since Hilary and I kept out of each other's way, so was I.

"Do you ever tell him you're not happy?" Andy asked.

"Yes, but when I do he says he gives me everything and refuses to see that I have reasons to be unhappy. When *he* is satisfied with what he's given, he feels that *I* should be satisfied as well. I think that sometimes he feels I am being immature because I can't be happy."

"Sometimes when you're with an older person, they treat you like *they* know what's best for you, and you don't know your own mind. He's too old for you. You should have someone younger."

"Yeah, maybe. I don't know. Sometimes I think that I've spent such a long time with him, that things would *definitely* be changing soon. I keep waiting for *soon*, but 'soon' gets further and further away."

"And you feel like you've wasted all that time so you might as well stay. But the longer you stay, the more time you invest and the harder it gets to leave," Andy continued.

"Exactly!" I agreed. "And he is so possessive, I can't talk to anyone. It's gotten to the point where I am afraid to go out with him because every single time we go out, he finds some reason to come back angry and I can't stand it anymore."

"Why is it so difficult to leave?"

"Well, because I feel like I'm leaving my home. I've carefully picked the things we have. When I moved in, we had nothing. It was a house. Now it's a beautiful home, lovingly made. From one pot I found in a dog kennel, we now have several. We have vases, radios and pictures on the wall – homey things. Even my home with my mum and sister doesn't feel the same. I didn't pick out and design the things they have."

"You don't want to leave the stuff you built up."

"Well, it's not about the *stuff*. I grew up poor. I already know that I can survive on very little 'stuff.'

Andy laughed.

"What?" I asked.

"I just like the way you look at it."

"Look at what?"

"Your attitude to *stuff*. One can easily say that if you grew up poor, you'd want *more* stuff, not the other way around."

"I don't know. I mean, if you know you don't need stuff to be happy, that's a big weight off your shoulders. Don't get me wrong, he's not a bad guy. He took me travelling the entire country and opened my eyes to so many things. I even had dinner with the new President."

"Really? With the President? What was that like?"

"You won't believe this. I was *so* embarrassed. The President said to me, 'Anne, you look beautiful tonight' and I was so nervous, I said, 'Yes, thanks you.' Yes *thanks* you!"

Andy laughed heartily, and I joined in. "I mean, who says, 'yes thanks you' when someone pays them a compliment. Luckily, not many people heard," I said. "I'll never forget that."

"I am sure you can find someone better, someone to give you everything you deserve, not just stuff," Andy said finally.

"You think that'll happen?"

"Look. See those blokes over there?"

"Where?"

"There, those blokes that run the water ski thingies."

"Oh yeah," I answered. They were on the beach every day, helping people with their water skis.

"They look at you all the time. I think they want to talk to you. You're beautiful – and that's without any make-up. You won't find a hard time finding someone good," Andy said.

"I don't really wear make-up, except for lipstick *sometimes*," I replied. I thought of all the times I'd put lipstick on, then wiped it off again. I always looked at myself in the mirror before going out with Razor, just to make sure I couldn't possibly elicit any male attention.

"So how come I *never* see the ski guys looking at me?" I asked Andy.

"Don't know," he answered, smiling. "*I* see them looking at you, when you walk past. I stare at them until they see me and look away."

"I have to go. I don't want to, but I have to. It's my turn to do dinner for Hilary and me." I said.

"Is it getting easier?" Andy asked.

"No, but it's the least I can do in a bad situation. I mean, he brought me here and I wouldn't have been able to experience all this without him," I said, pointing to the clear sea and the clean white sand. "He's a really, really good guy. Trust me, I know."

"Sounds like you've had some bad experiences."

"Well, sort of," I answered. I shivered, remembering some of the tight scrapes I had gotten out of.

"See you tomorrow?" Andy asked.

"Sure."

"I have to go into the city in the morning, but I'll be down here by mid-day."

"Bye, Andy."

"Bye, Anne."

"Why do you always wrap yourself so tightly with your towel before you come up the cottage?" Hilary asked when I walked in.

"It just feels like the right thing to do," I answered.

"You let *him* see you in your swim suit. Why not me?"

"Who?" I said with my back turned so he couldn't see the panic on my face. We had never been on the beach together, and the day he took me into the city, he left me on a corner and picked me up half an hour later.

"That guy you sit and talk to," he answered.

"You watched me?" I asked, scared that he might say yes.

"The cottage is right across the road from the beach. I just walked over to see what you got up to all day when you're out there. You don't even come in for lunch sometimes."

"What *could* I get up to on a public beach?" I asked guiltily, not knowing why I *felt* any guilt at all.

"So tell me. Who is he?" Hilary asked.

"He's just a guy. We met when he saved my life. I can't swim and I was paddling in the shallow water, which suddenly went over my head when a big wave came in. We started talking and we became friends. That's all. We're just friends."

"Where is he from?" Hilary asked, still not satisfied. I had a feeling he didn't believe me.

"He's from Manchester in England. Here on holiday."

"On his own?"

"Yes. He's staying at a friend's house. They live back in England," I answered.

"I bet he's invited you over there already?"

"Just for a game of cards, but I told him I couldn't come."

I neglected to say that I smuggled the little books Andy lent me in my towel so that I wouldn't be asked any questions about them. Or that we'd exchanged addresses and promised to keep in touch after we got back home.

"I know those guys from Manchester. They're not all they seem. He wouldn't let you use his towel if he was only interested in a game of cards," Hilary said angrily.

"So you saw that?" I asked. Andy had lent me his towel when mine got a bit wet. He didn't go anywhere for lunch either. He sat with me until I left.

Hillary needn't answer. But the way he downed his head told me that he was ashamed. The towel incident happened days ago, so he must have been watching us since then.

I wondered how much time he was spending with his family, if he was around the beach cottage all day watching *me*. Hillary had no reason to be ashamed, though. I was the one at fault. I was the one who took his plane ticket, turned up and didn't fall in love with him like he expected. *I* was the one who should be ashamed.

"I'm sorry," I said. "You're a good, decent guy. You deserve someone who loves you for you – someone who would fall head over heels in love with you. I know you'll treat the right woman very well. Just three more days and I'll be out of your hair, then you can move back home and spend the rest of your holidays there."

I cooked dinner in silence and was almost tempted to go out for a little walk on the beach but I didn't. Tomorrow I would soak up everything I saw, so that I could save the good memories of this beautiful haven called Barbados.

But when tomorrow came it wasn't a day for going out. The morning started with a torrent of rain and when I got ready for the beach Hilary told me I would be crazy going out there.

"This is a hurricane," he said. "No one will be on the beach, not even your 'boyfriend.'"

It was my first *honest* hurricane. I saw waves as high as houses all the way from across the street. We had to keep the radio on, as the officials were considering evacuating houses within two hundred yards of the beach.

I sat at the window and watched the palm trees twist crazily in the storm. The area that was yesterday crawling with people, had become a ghost town overnight. Hilary was right. No one in his right mind would go to the beach today.

I was cheated out of a day, a precious day of nearly happiness. And in some strange way, I was missing Andy. I had some big decisions to make when I got home. There was going to be some huge changes in my life and most of them not for the better, or maybe they were.

The time had come for me to cash in my bad investment. I should bow out at zero, rather than wait until I was in the red.

I was happier living in poverty with my mum and sister, borrowing Sasha's clothes, and eating next to nothing. Life was good then.

Why did God make us like this? Why did the things we need most like love and loyalty have to come from other people?

The next two days sped up on a fast forward button. The day before I left, I went to say a very painful goodbye to my good-listener friend.

"I have a solution, Anne," Andy said when he saw me.

"What, a solution to my life?" I smiled.

"Sorry. I've been practising this all the way over here and the first thing I said didn't make sense!"

"No, I was only joking, really. What do you have a solution to?"

"Okay, listen, you know I'm staying in a cottage nearby, right? There are four bedrooms, two on each side of the cottage. I phoned the owners last night and asked if I could have a friend stay with me and they said it was okay. I'll go with you over to your cottage and help you pack. I'll stand with you – whatever you want to tell your guy. You can move in with me and stay for a bit longer. We can go change your ticket and all that. You have my word that I will stay on one side of the cottage and give you the other. You can trust me . . ."

"Andy," I cut in. "I *know* I can trust you. After I met a really nice older guy some years back, I promised myself I wouldn't judge all men based on the ugly, nasty ones. I trust you completely. . ."

"But . . ." Andy sensed I had a *but* – a big one.

"I can't do that to Hillary. He's been really great, a real gentleman. Never touched me. He bought me food, took me to the city centre and stuff. I could never forgive myself if I treated a good person that way – even though I want nothing better than to stay here longer."

"I was so looking forward to getting to know you better, Anne."

"Me too."

"Do we shake hands, hug?" Andy asked.

"I'd like a hug, please."

His hug released the tears in me and I tried desperately to hold them in. I didn't want to pay attention to the nagging feeling that I'd fallen for this man who'd saved my life.

"I wish you didn't have to go," he said, but his voice was muffled, coming from a long way away. "There are so many things I've waited too late to say."

I wanted to rest my head in his chest, but I was worried about Hillary. If he saw our innocent hug, there would be no way I could convince him that we were not 'up to something.'

"Thank you for saving my life," I said as dredged up all the strength I could find to pull away. "Write to me, okay."

I walked away without looking back. When I got to the road and glanced back, Andy was a lonely six-foot-four, sunburnt figure in the distance. He waved and I waved back.

A Guyanese proverb: Wha sweet a goat mouth a bitter a he bambam.

Translation: The very thing that's sweet to a goat's mouth, is bitter when it reaches his behind (literally - cayenne peppers).

Meaning: Sometimes the very thing that seems to you pleasure will bring you pain in the end.

CHAPTER 35 – BACK HOME?

"I was so scared you weren't coming back," Razor said. "I'm really glad you did."

I felt I wouldn't have the courage to say I was leaving him (almost), but I shut my eyes and had the talk. The following day I was on a mini bus travelling back to New Amsterdam.

All my life I've wanted to be loved, but I was walking away from three versions of it, leaving the house I loved and called home for so long.

The trip back was slow, hot and dreadful. As always, the sound of Buju Banton, Shaggy and Chakademus blared on the speakers in the packed mini-bus. These singers made a living poking fun at women, boasting of their conquests in every smut-compilation they called a 'song.' This was *not* what I wanted to hear going back. It reminded me too much of the things I thought I'd left behind. It made me question my decisions over the last week in Barbados.

Suddenly an almighty bang roused me from my deep thoughts, almost making me jump out of my skin. The driver swerved crazily on the narrow road. Everyone girlie-screamed and gripped the seat in front of them, preparing to meet their maker. With none of the twenty-four people travelling in the eighteen-seater wearing a seat-belt, we reeled dangerously forward, before the driver managed to screech to a standstill.

"We hit a sheep! Is alrite!" the driver cried. With the slowing traffic behind us, he quickly jumped out, looked at the front of his bus, took a slight intake of breath, piled the dead sheep in the back, and promptly drove off.

"Curry mutton tonight!" he chuckled at his conductor who was trying to recompose his swagger after being pancake-tossed face first into the window of the bus.

I wondered what it would feel like three weeks later, when I was planning to make this trip again to pick up the rest of my personal stuff. Having to move with a public mini bus, must be the single, most destroying way to do it.

When the mini-bus ride was over, I still had a delayed ferry trip across the wide, Berbice river, and a long walk home, carrying bags that were as big as me around.

Finally, when I got home, Errol was sitting on the scrubbed bench outside our front door. His desperate love for his mother-in-law had long since dried up to spittle. His visiting companion was now his brother-in-law. I couldn't even look at his face.

"I need you. Please come back," was the first thing Razor said to me when I walked back into the home I'd created from his skeleton house. It felt empty, but the maid had kept it clean.

"It didn't work before. Won't work now," I answered, getting my things together.

"Are you kidding? You took me out of the kennel I was living in for years, when you took that pot out of the doghouse. That pot is *my* freedom. Look at this house, your home. Come, let me show you something."

Razor led the way to the kitchen, took the old dog pot off the dresser where it stood like a pot of fresh flowers in a crystal vase, and put it in my hand.

"What does this mean to you?" he asked, with tears in his eyes. I thought for a moment and realised that for me it meant a beginning of something new. It was this feeling of hope and renewal that consumed my senses, not the feeling of misery and disillusionment I felt when I left three weeks ago.

"Don't go back and leave me. Let's bring your stuff back. *I'll* bring them back. We'll do it together."

"You know you get mobbed when you go to New Amsterdam," I answered weakly.

"I don't care. I'll be mobbed for *you*. Just say you'll stay."

"Will you change your possessive ways? Will you stop getting angry when I say I want to go out to work?" I asked, hoping he'd say yes.

"I'll do anything. You know I could give you *everything*. You don't have to work. I take care of your family . . ."

"You see! This is why. . ."

"Okay, Okay."

"You give me what you *want* to give me – fancy clothes so I look good on your arm, lots of shoes . . . material things. What about loyalty and stability and all the stuff money can't buy?" I cried.

"I'll be the person you want me to be," Razor answered. "I can't lose you. You're pure and innocent and that keeps me from losing my soul completely. I need your calm because it makes me feel like a good person again – and I'm *not* a good person. It's hard for me to live with myself without your innocence."

"I think you mean my *naivety*," I said. "I'll stay, but only if you mean what you say about changing. We have to go home soon because I took most of my shoes and books."

"*This* is your home. Why don't we go tomorrow?" Razor replied.

CHAPTER 35 – RAVINGS OF AN UNLACED HEART

Razor had just stepped out with a piece of newspaper under his arm, on the way to our latrine, which stood at the very back of the land on which we lived.

Miss Hyacinth had had her house built on Solly's family's land, which she had leased for twenty-five years. I guess when Solly's dad signed on the dotted line, he had no idea that she would live for so long.

The lease has been up for years, but Miss Hyacinth, not wanting to move, agreed that Solly's parents could take the house when she died.

I wondered how Solly was doing? I missed him. In fact, I missed all my dancing friends. Razor had a terrible motorcycle accident in his youth, which left one leg slightly shorter than the other – not a good combination for dancing, which meant I didn't do it anymore.

Of all the things I missed, going to church was at the top of the list.

That emptiness left me feeling like I'd used a tea strainer to drain bits of my soul, leaving an empty bucket where it used to be. For someone who used to be an altar boy, Razor hated priests.

"My parents and the seven of us kids used to sit in the front row," he said to me once.

"I thought you were dirt poor."

"Oh, yeah," he replied, "We were, but our colour matched the priest's so we got a free ride. I saw my black friends and their old grannies with their little head-ties standing in the back. Stretch, it made a hole right here." Razor put his hand to his heart. "And you know what else I hated?"

"What?" I had asked him. I knew he had a lot more to say than he was telling me.

"I hated it how the parents trusted those guys dressed up, prancing about in their robes. They left their boys with them like it was nothing, and as soon as the parents were out the door, they found some reason to take the boys to the vestry."

"I know what it feels like to find out you have to be scared of someone you didn't *know* you had to be afraid of," I told him. "It hurts even more."

"Exactly. If you *knew* you had to be wary of them, at least you'd keep your guard up."

"I see your point with the trust thing," I said. "I have a problem with outward rituals of water blessings and stone kissing. I just don't feel they add up to the true sense of the bible."

Razor had a lot more to say about the poor, black grannies standing in the back behind the last pews. His pain made me reflect on what I'd been thinking about lately, the things I no longer wanted to do.

After all, if I worshipped and held reverent something I or another human could *make* with our hands, weren't *we* the greater ones in this twisted God-man relationship?

Didn't I read that God created man? And if the Bible is my foundation of belief and I accept it as my source of spiritual wisdom, shouldn't I believe what it says when it tells me that God hates idolatry and that He dwells not in a building but in my heart? Therefore, which is the holy place, my *heart* or the sacristy?

After Razor had walked out whistling to the latrine in our back yard, Mum handed me a letter with a postmark from England.

My trembling hands could barely tear the thin envelope because I recognised the sender's name instantly.

I was the least superstitious person I knew, but I wondered why Andy's letter had arrived on the day I was going back.

Now I'm back home, it said, *I still think of you every day. I know this will come as a shock, so forgive me if I'm speaking out of turn. I know now that I don't want to remain just friends. I've fallen in love with you. Please say I can visit you. I miss you terribly and can't bear not seeing you every day . . .*

I read the letter twice before Razor walked back into our little home, the one my uncle Daniel called a garage. I would keep it close to me and read it a dozen times each day, but for now, I had to tear myself away.

Razor sat in the new chair I'd bought, as I stuffed the letter back into its envelope. I looked at him and saw a man totally at peace with himself and the world, and knew I was making the right decision for him.

Yes, it *was* the right decision. I fiercely hoped to see Andy again, and even though I knew it would *never* happen, I found that hoping took the edge off the pain.

If I had realised that Andy and I felt that way about each other, would I have come back? But I refused to even think about it, let alone allow myself to answer.

Three weeks later, I had an interview at the University of Guyana. One week after that I had a job.

Two weeks after *that,* Razor and I were arguing again. One afternoon, so angry that I was an hour late (my mini-bus didn't show up), he threw a tantrum and kept at it well into the night. In the quiet surroundings of the private neighbours, his powerful voice seemed to echo for miles through the open windows.

Finally, embarrassment got the better of me. I figured that he couldn't shout at someone he couldn't see. I picked up a pillow and a blanket and walked out the door.

I didn't do 'tension' very well. I needed to get through the rest of the night in peace in order to have a clear space to think tomorrow. The most important thing was getting to the back garden without being seen under the scrutiny of the neighbours' security lights illuminating every inch of space.

Because we were friends, I didn't want Lora to see me. She was the au pair of the world-travellers who lived nearby. Sometimes when Razor was at work, Lisa and I spent time with her. Lora had access to the family's endless supply of marijuana and thought it polite to offer me first smoke whenever we visited.

"It won't do no harm. Cathy and Malcolm do it all the time," she said each time I refused, as if her wealthy, foreign employers were the standard by which we should live.

"That thing sends you crazy," I tell her. "I went to school near the asylum, and we saw first-hand what rolling the leaves did to people's lives.

I know people who went off their heads after smoking that stuff."

"You can't go mad the *first* time," Lora says.

"Well, I never want to find out. I might be *the* person who does."

Once we'd gone through this ritual-greeting, we could move onto other things.

To Razor, I was disloyal because I had a life away from him. It was as if going out of his sight meant that I was cheating in a fashion only understood by his broken web of thinking.

With nothing but a nightgown between my bony body and the hard ground, I lay down and covered myself with the blanket.

I didn't know it then, but sleeping on the dry ground was preparing me for years later, when at college I had nowhere to live, and for four months, had to sleep on a wooden floor with nothing but a thin sheet between me and the floorboards.

Mum always said that I should put some flesh on my bones. Maybe she was right. Some extra layers of flesh can come in quite handy for sleeping on dry ground.

I almost laughed out loud at this. Lying on my back made my protruding spine hurt. Turning over made my hinge-like hipbones grate against the ground. I wondered how many pounds of flesh it would take to cover those up. Who was it that was asked for a pound of flesh? Was it Shakespeare's Antonio who was supposed to give it to Shylock or the other way around?

The slight, wayward thoughts cleared my head somewhat. Before falling to painful sleep, I had a clear plan.

Tomorrow after work, I would go see Aunt B (my Uncle Compton's partner) and ask her to take me in.

I said my prayer before dozing off, the one I said before I went to sleep. *Lord help me to find the right path to you, because I don't think I am on it.*

A Guyanese Proverb: If yuh eye na see, yuh mouth shouldn't taak.

Translation: If your eye didn't see, your mouth shouldn't speak.

Meaning: If you didn't witness something, you shouldn't talk about it as if it's true. Beware of gossiping people.

CHAPTER 36 – MOVING ON OUT

Staying with Aunt B and Uncle Compton in Paradise was apt not only because of the name of the village, but also because I was wrapped – covered in their acceptance.

Of course, Aunt B already had her sons, her brother and his pregnant girlfriend, and *my* brother there. (*The pregnant girlfriend is one of my first cousins. She's not related to Aunt B's brother, as Aunt B is not our blood relative*).

They had a full three-bedroom house, with eight (soon to be nine) of us all crammed in, but the laughter and fun oiled us so well, there was no rough place left for friction.

Each night was like crashing at a friend's after a house party, where everyone was having too much fun to bother going home.

Of course, I did a lot of housework, and carried water for the home with the boys. I washed the high-traffic floors when I came home from work, and if it rained – again before bedtime. But unlike Uncle Daniel's household, my efforts were appreciated. And when I had to do it again ten minutes later (especially after the baby was born), it was appreciated all over again.

There was always a relative going and another (or two) coming; babies being born; practical jokes being pulled; pots of food to be cooked; children's screams to ignore; outings to be planned; and visits to be made.

I wondered where I would be, and what my journey would've been like, had I known Uncle Compton all my life.

His Tapir van, the only vehicle we had to get into the city (where he, my dad, my sisters and I worked) broke down almost every morning, right when we were about to leave for work.

Ten-year-old Mikey was great at fixing it and driving it to the gate at the end of the pathway, where we piled in (sometimes sitting on each other's laps) and went off to work and school.

At night, I slept in the bottom bunk of the child-sized bed in the hallway, my ankle and feet hanging off the edge, but since this was all happening on the outskirts of heaven, *nothing* could be better.

In the countryside, the Bluesakies and the Kiskadees woke me up every morning, whistling their merry tunes, perched in the nearby fruit trees. City living had made me forget just how much I missed that kind of music.

Our house was at the front of an extensive property. My father, Sue and another sister lived in the large house at the back with 'Aunty' Sheila. Aunty Sheila owned everything, including the prosperous baker-shop on the far side of her land, the goats, sheep, poultry and abundant fruit trees.

Why didn't *I* live there instead of in my cramped conditions? I don't know; maybe I just never asked.

I did live with them at a later stage when I was at college full-time. After a few months, 'Aunty' Sheila got tired of me and chucked me out. I don't know if Dad tried to fight for me, but I had Aunty B and Uncle Compton on my side, who again, took me in. By then there were also four little kids living in the house. (My family knows how to breed).

After a few months when 'Aunty' Sheila gave them notice to move, we all had to find somewhere else to go – separating the household temporarily. This is when I ended up sleeping in the corner of an empty bedroom, in Aunty B's distant relative's house.

Then I hit a sudden brick wall in Paradise. I watched the splintered bits of reality come crushing down around my feet. I simply could not go on working at the University.

My wages were a lot less than the money I needed *just* to survive. My financial contribution towards my new family was little, but it was enough to lessen the amount I could send for Mum and Franc. I lived as cheaply as possible. I altered my formal clothes and wore them to work, and got a lift there in my uncle's tapir.

Each day I thought of what I could drop in order to stay and work. I skipped breakfast, then breakfast *and* lunch.

I had an idea I could walk back home and even tried it one day, but conked out halfway. Neither my body nor I could take it any longer, especially when the pounds fell off me like dead skin.

The only reason I stayed for as long as I did was because my large family was so good to me and Aunt B was so beautiful and supportive. I just *had* to go back home. I still had some of my personal things at Razor's house and when I went with my cousin to pick them up, he offered to help me but wanted me to stay. I couldn't and didn't.

CHAPTER 37 – BACK IN THE SMALL TOWN

It took me a while but I managed, despite the constant lull in the employment market to secure a job at Guymine, the bauxite mines where my father worked for most of his life.

I'd applied for the job about two years ago after I left Matt Peters. The vacancy, filled then, had come back around full circle.

An apparition in the form of a Land Rover turned up in our street one day. Apart from the taxis, which picked up the prostitutes, people who could afford to drive a vehicle stayed well away.

Everyone in the area watched as the Land Rover manoeuvred the giant-sized manholes in the brick-and-gravel surface. Maybe there was a tarred road a generation ago, but only tiny pockets of the asphalt were still visible.

Remarkably, the vehicle stopped outside our yard, and the guy in the passenger seat asked one of the half-dressed children playing in the street to run to the back and get me.

"You Anne Lyken?" he asked.

"Yes. Who's asking?"

"You remember a good while back, you applied for a job at Guymine?" he asked.

"Yes. That was a couple years ago," I answered. "You've come to offer me the job?" I joked, knowing he would laugh and tell me not to be silly. It wasn't strange that someone from Personnel had turned up outside my yard. The odd thing was that I desperately needed a job *at that minute.*

"That's why I'm here," he said, making my jaw hang loose. "It's yours if you still want it."

I was one of twelve temporary stocktaking clerks. Guymine sent their buses into town every two hours – all day. All I had to do was hop on at a stop near home, and ride into the mines. The Personnel, Finance, Warehouse employees *and* miners all travelled together, and everyone seemed to get along fine.

My twelve-hour shifts (from eight to eight), six days a week, paid adequately, and finally, I could take care of my family.

I was satisfied I had my independence, even though from the outside it looked like I had no life.

It was while I was resting on our bench outside, one Sunday afternoon, that I first heard his story. Two of Miss Bessy's daughters were deep in conversation, their naked children, resting on their laps.

I had my back turned to them, and didn't look around, but they were discussing the front house in our yard and my ears pricked up.

I had been practically living at work for the past five months, so knew none of the most recent gossip bulletins flying around. I woke at sunrise to prepare for the forty-five minutes' drive to work, then returned after dark, when I often met Mum and Franc outside the ice-cream shop (they walked from home to meet me there) to spend my over-time chits on fresh bread and ice-cream.

"How long he been living in Elaine's house?" asked voice One.

"Too long," replied voice Two. "How can a man be so stupid, eh? Nuff people would kill to be where he was, and look what he gone and do,"

"Is all dem dope he smoke. It turn him mad," voice One agreed. "When you in a foreign country, yuh got to be very careful. They doan want no Guyanese criminals in their jails. They post you right back here, with handcuffs on the plane and everything."

"Ah hear that he spend time in the Canadian prison first," Two said. "And when they deported him, he come off the plane with two policemen side by side of him. It's only when he stepped on the ground that them take the handcuffs off."

"What a shame on the family!" One exclaimed. "If Elaine was still here, she would never allow him to stay in the house with she."

I realised early in the conversation that they were talking about the young man who had moved into the front house Solly's family owned.

On my return home, I had so much stuff, I had to move into a bedroom in the front house for a while. As time went by, working in the mines all day (even though I was in a Warehouse) took its toll on the clothes I *could* wear to work.

Temporary workers weren't entitled to the company's popular steel-fronted work shoes, so I wore my high heels until the bauxite on the ground ate them up. I took them to the cobblers as long as they had enough good leather left to repair. And when they were beyond help, I stuck them together with nails and thumb tacks, many of which bore into my feet with each step, leaving permanent scar tissue and discolouration to remind me of the time I spent with them. In time, I had only one pair left.

Duncan, Solly's cousin moved into the front house while I was still there. By then, Donna and her daughter, having found out that her knight in shining armour was *never* going to ride up, had skipped town.

Duncan's bedroom was at one end, mine at the other. He had emigrated young enough to be left with no trace of a local accent. He had one little bag when he arrived at the house, carrying nothing but a change of clothes and a Canadian twang.

"Them girls gone still flock him, though," voice One was saying, "With that fancy Canadian accent and them good looks, he'll soon be the best catch around."

"What kinda girl gon want a man with no job and no money?" Two asked. He's half a man with him ganja brains."

"He come from Canada! That's all them girls wanna know," One answered. "He mother still there and he might get things in the post now and then. Yuh know them girls like foreign things!" They both laughed hysterically.

"Yuh right, yuh know. They won't care that he's a murderer."

The last word made me sit up and take notice. Did I actually share a house with a murderer? Duncan was reasonably behaved, even when he was high. He never smoked in the house, and listened intently to my advice about anger management and psychology knick-knacks. He waited in the dark kitchen most nights, and when I came through the front door, he emerged, asking after my health before diving in with questions about his problems.

As far as I knew, Duncan never came near my bedroom, something which, in my book, had put him above Jerry Saunders and his gang.

CHAPTER 38 – THE PROMOTION

I started dating Cyril about four months into working at Guymine. I wasn't going for anything serious – just half a dozen walks up the Back Dam Road, and one date to the cinema.

When the stocktaking in the back warehouse came to the end, three of us were promoted to the main Finance building at the front of the mines, as Dual-Accounting Clerks.

We were beside ourselves with joy – no more walking through the damp bauxite dust to the old, dusty warehouse for us! With our new, steel-tipped shoes and raise in pay I, Afzal, and Donald were walking with the big boys from the buses, to the pavement, straight into the plush Finance building, to our special, private D.A room!

Oh, the three of us now had to dress differently! We were rubbing shoulders with the bad boys who had their claws firmly around the billion-dollar mine's purse (the ones with private transportation and their own chauffeurs).

Our job description was secret to most of the finance underdogs until we showed up all proud and puffed out.

"What y'all doing?" they all knocked on our D.A office door to ask. We must have explained our task a dozen times. We were converting the cost of every asset – from the tiniest of bolts to the largest of the mine's transport barges, from Guyanese to U.S dollars.

"So is true that we gon be taken over by an American company?" they asked. We didn't know, but then again, we weren't important enough to be given such details. The donkeywork was ours and we did it with braying delight.

I changed abode from the warehouse at the back, to the shiny finance offices in front. Everyone went home at four in the afternoon, but Afzal, Donald and I kept working into the night, most times being supervised (from their private office down the corridor) by either of our two foremen.

Cyril popped into my office several times a day for a chat at the start. The first time he asked me out, I told Afzal, who was by then my best friend. His response startled me. "Don't do it," he said, "Ah think he's going out with Karen from Payroll. At least wait and I'll try to find out for you."

So I waited and made silly excuses to Cyril for two weeks. Afzal was mistaken. Surely, if two people from the same department were a couple, they would have lunch together, or at least *speak* to each other when we played card games at lunch?

"Are you going out with Karen?" I asked Cyril one day – in front of Afzal.

"Yuh kidding, right?" he asked, indignant. "What would I do with such an ugly girl? Yuh know what she looks like, right?"

"You don't have to be nasty about her," I said. "Only asking coz I was told the two of you're a couple."

I looked over to Afzal's desk opposite mine; ignoring the fist he waved at me, and continued, "By a reliable source."

"Well, tell your *source*," Cyril answered. "They got it wrong. I would never go out with someone like Karen. She is not my type at all."

For the next six weeks, Cyril and I planned to meet up sometimes after I finished work. I was always tired and wasn't interested in much else than a stroll. Cyril was always adamant that walking past the middle of the town (which took less than ten minutes) was too much for him.

"You're home by five o'clock," I said to him. "Why're *you* so tired?"

Once, we went to the cinema house on my side of town, even though the movie I wanted to see was showing at The Strand, which was on other half of town.

The six weeks of casually dating Cyril got increasingly stranger. On two occasions, I spotted him with friends as I walked home from the ice-cream shop (which was in the other half of town) with Mum and Franc. When I looked back to wave at him, he turned his head, pretending to be deep in conversation with his pal.

I had a feeling the deep involvement was fake, but I gave him the benefit of the doubt and walked on.

The month of Ramadan came around for Afzal and he brought several bags of food to work, food his mother had woken up when it was still dark to cook.

Afzal left his desk seven times a day to wash in the basins at work and say his prayers. Still in his cheerful way, he insisted that Cyril was seeing Karen. *I* insisted – while eating some of his mother's fabulous cooking he shared with me when he broke fast at six – that he assured me he wasn't.

"I believe you *think* you're right, Afzal. But you *must* have the wrong information," I told him. "Cyril or no other man would pursue so strongly, someone in the same building where his 'girlfriend' worked. This alone makes me believe he's telling the truth."

"Listen, Anne," this was how Afzal began his responses to me, even if he was about to tell me a joke.

"No, Afzal, *you* listen. Why would Cyril *keep* asking me to be his girlfriend and run the risk of Karen finding out if he was *already* with her? You haven't yet answered that basic question. Besides, the things he's said about her, no one would say about the girl he's with."

Afzal reminded me of the friends I had in the past, friends who made me feel good and perfect inside; people like Dave and Brian (who left the country while I was in the city without saying goodbye).

"Listen, Anne," Afzal said again. "Yuh know how *some* people are when it comes to going overseas. Yuh know that Karen's mum is sending for her to go to Canada, right?" *Right* was another of Afzal's favourite words.

"Right?" he repeated, waiting for me to answer.

"Yes, yes."

"Well, maybe Cyril's just keeping Karen sweet so when she goes away she will send him a free ticket out of the country." Afzal stopped working, walked over to my desk, and handed me another of his puluries, with the bowl of extra-thick tamarind sour.

"Thanks," I said. "This is really good. Does your mum make this tamarind sour as well?"

"Yeah, but she always packs too much stuff. Good thing I got you to sniff it up," Afzal joked.

"You think someone could be so cruel, though?" I asked finally. "I don't think he could. I'm really sure of that, Afzal."

"Listen, Anne. Listen to me, right," Afzal said, again leaving his dual accounting chart on his desk and walking over. As long as we worked all day, no one cared about how much food we consumed or what we listened to on our radio. "Me cousin at The Strand cinema said he saw them two there."

"I believe you, Afzal," I told him again. "But I don't believe your cousin. Cyril has no stake in this. We're not girlfriend and boyfriend. *He's* pursuing *me*. Why would he put all that energy into lying when there's nothing to gain from it? He wouldn't' *lose* anything with me, because he's getting nothing from me."

"What's the matter, Anne!" someone was shouting in my ear. "Wake up! Wake up!" The room was spinning around and I was falling . . . falling.

"Listen, Anne!" the voice shouted again. "You took the tablets didn't you, you fool!" After that, I woke up in hospital.

"What happened?" I asked Afzal, when I came to. His face was so close to mine, his long hair batted my forehead.

"I told yuh not to take Bailey's stupid tablets."

"But they were just strong pain killers, weren't they?" I asked. Neither the boys nor I had

occasionally came in and spoke to me. Surely, that was proof if I ever needed any.

We got the sad news one day at work. By then my crazy Dual-Accounting days were behind me, and I went home at four with everyone else. Karen's father had been ill for some time, and he died quietly in his sleep. Her mum and little sister were flying in from Canada for the funeral.

Cyril and I turned up together at their house the night before the funeral for the 'wake.' We hadn't planned it. We just happened to run into each other in the street and walked in together.

With the other mourners, we sat on a bench under Karen's house, playing dominos and card games. About ten in the evening, I couldn't find Karen when I looked around for her to say goodbye. Oddly enough, Cyril had also disappeared. I spoke to her brother and left for home.

Their street was pitch black in the blackout night, but in the moon light, I could make out two figures about 100 yards ahead. I instinctively knew who they were, and for some odd reason, felt, above all, relieved.

Karen and Cyril were so engrossed in their argument they didn't see me come up. "We only met in the street," he was saying to her.

"You expect me to believe you?" she asked, tears in her voice.

He grabbed her by the elbow and she pulled away, turning towards me, almost bumping into me in the dark.

"Good night," I said to both of them. I didn't stop to pay my respects because I knew if there was an awful time to do so, that was it.

Ironically, Cyril for once in his life, was telling the truth, but was being called a liar for it.

I resolved I wasn't going to let him talk himself out of this one. In fact, I wasn't even going to ask him for an explanation. A man who would argue with his girlfriend – which I now believed she was – in her time of grief was no man at all.

"Karen," I said when we met a week later. "There isn't a worse time to ask you this, but I have to. Are you and Cyril together?"

"Yes," Karen smiled calmly, as if she was relieved that *I* was the one who asked. "We've been in a serious relationship for the last two years."

I told her everything – apart from the derogatory names he'd called her. No woman deserved to know that her boyfriend had tried to woo another woman by saying she was too ugly to be 'competition.'

The more we talked, the more we found out. She and I lived on opposite sides of the small town. He'd told her he hated the cinema near me, and hadn't gone there with *her* in the last six weeks. When they went for walks, he never crossed the so-called middle line.

No wonder he didn't go to the Strand cinema with me. So Afzal's cousin was right! When I was working late, he spent the afternoon with her while I was still at work. By the time *I* got home, he had time enough to have dinner and a shower, and was free to visit me.

Karen and I worked out that he came to my desk when she was out of the office, something I hadn't noticed before. He did the same to her when *I* wasn't there.

"Karen," I said, at last, "This is my decision. I'm *never* talking to him again. I find it laughable that he could *believe* we're so stupid. I don't mind what you decide to do, but I'm out of his mess."

"I can't laugh at it, Anne. But I'm done with him too. He wanted to hold onto both of us, now he's got nothing."

"I am really glad we're not attacking each other, Karen. That is the most important thing," I answered.

The next day Cyril came boldly to my desk (when Karen had stepped out – I made note of it this time).

"Go away. I have nothing to say to you." I told him. My decision about him was final.

"Wait, you're angry *just* because you saw me talking to Karen last night? We were just . . ."

"Go away!" I said, louder this time. *He was still making excuses – still trying to lie.* This time, the other people in the office stared at him and he left.

I never spoke to Cyril again, not even to ask for an explanation. I didn't need one. Two weeks later, Karen was back with him. She and I remained friends and continued to work alongside each other. Cyril never came into the office again, but opted to meet her outside in secret – just like before, making her into his invisible girlfriend once more.

Oddly, I didn't feel hurt. I felt empowered – strong that I could walk away from Cyril and our handful of dates without feeling let down. The one thing I knew for sure was that I was done with dating in my town. If Cyril was anything to go by – and he was, a 'girlfriend' meant nothing. All of my indignation was for Karen. I felt none for myself. For me, all I felt was incredulity, with a slice of laughter, at his desperation.

A Guyanese Proverb: New broom sweep clean, but old wan noo de karna.

Translation: A new broom sweeps clean, but an old one knows the corners.

Meaning: do not ignore your old friends when new ones come along. New friends may be fun, but the old ones know you better and will be there for you in difficult situations.

CHAPTER 39 – HELP NEEDED

"Anne! Anne! Help!" Darla shouted. My name rolled off the tip of her tongue whenever she was in a tight squeeze. I was meant to be going to a play rehearsal, but when Darla shouted for help, she was in a life-threatening situation.

Today, Duncan was holding the machete to her neck as he pinned her to the wall of the cramped, smelly, borrowed bedroom they called home. Richard, the tiny, extremely malnourished baby I named and often looked after, was lying in the middle of the double bed in which the three of them slept. It was the only piece of furniture in the room – well, unless one could call the bundles of clothes piled on the floor *furnishing*.

"I'll kill her, Anne! I'll kill her right now! I have no use for her!" Duncan shouted, his Canadian accent ripping through the almost tangible smell of urine in the bedroom, and Richard's mournful, hungry wails.

Darla moved in with Duncan about a year ago, a week after meeting him. Whether it was because of his Canadian accent, his ready smile or his confident charm, I couldn't say. Miss Bessy's daughters had made it their business to tell her about his deportation, but Darla was in love.

Two months later, she told me she was pregnant, when I stopped to talk to her after work. She and Duncan occupied the back bedroom (within screaming distance of our place) of the front house, while a family of six lived in the rest of the three-bedroomed house. They shared use of the kitchen, but with Duncan's minimum wage as a load carrier, and with his marijuana habit, Darla's use of the kitchen was limited to nightfall only, as this was when Duncan returned with whatever he could squeeze out of his few dollars' earnings.

At nineteen, Darla was just a couple of years younger than me. She ignored my advice about going back home to her parents. She knew she could just shout for me when Duncan beat her with whatever he had in his hand – including his fists.

"You and the baby have nothing to eat all day. You can't raise a kid like this," I said. "What's keeping you here, Darla?"

"He really nice when he not high, Anne. Ah got a baby now. I got to stick with he. Besides, not everyone's like yuh. *I* would get lonely."

"Why not let her go, Duncan. Are you willing to get into trouble for her too?" I asked. I felt terrible talking about Darla as if she were merely a thing, but I had learnt from identical intimate dealings with him, this was the only way to make Duncan stop.

I had put my body between his and hers when he held his knife against her wrist and sliced into it repeatedly. I had breathlessly taken his cutlass from his hand several times, as he broadsided Darla with it, painting the bedroom walls with the spray of her blood. I'd spent more time closer to Duncan this past year, than I did when we lived in the same house. Back then, we sat on opposite sides of the living room to talk.

"Anne, let me explain." Duncan, for some reason, felt he had to explain his behaviour to me. I wasn't interested in his reasons, but the pause in action always gave me a chance to think of how to get him off her. The bed – in the middle of the room – was between them and me. I had to find a way to get to his hand before he did something fatal with it.

"This girl, this girl," he continued, with his free arm held tightly against Darla's throat, pressing her body into the wall. "She tests me. I got to show her Anne, that she can't test me and get away with it. She's got no respect, man. No respect!"

"I understand Duncan," I answered. "A man *does* need to be respected. I hear you loud and clear. But a man also needs to protect his girl, you know?" I slowly inched around the bed. "Just step away a little so we can talk this through, yeah?"

"I know what you want, Anne. You always want my machete!" Duncan cried with a snarl-smile. He was getting angrier, and for the first time in more than a year of knowing him, I was afraid of him turning on me.

"But, you ain't getting it this time, man," he continued, pointing the weapon at me. He closed his eyes and shook his head from side to side.

"No Duncan," I said, finally touching his tense, muscular, machete-holding arm. "What would I do with your machete? Just step away from Darla so we could cool off and have a chat." I backed away towards the door, hoping he would follow me.

Duncan stepped away from Darla, and I turned away slightly so he couldn't see me exhale. I was normally not scared of him, but Darla's spilled blood on his arms, made me think of a time when I saw myself bleeding down a drain.

Darla remained pinned to the wall in shock, as though he was *still* there. He walked past the bed, over to where I had moved towards the bedroom door, wiping the sweat off his forehead. Richard's wails were becoming more frantic, his naked, bony ribcage spasming dangerously. I realised that this was the part where I *had* to take action.

I slowly stepped on the outside of Duncan, keeping my eyes fixed on his, meaning to ask his permission to pick the baby up . . .

"Duncan, you monster! You stupid fool!" Darla shouted, awakening from her corner. Before I could react, Duncan lashed out across the bed with his cutlass with a broad-sider. In his steaming anger, his aim was a bit off and the tip of the blade cut through Darla's skin. Before I felt the wind on my face from the swing of Duncan's arm, the splatter of blood sprayed like rain over Richard's open mouth and makeshift nappy.

Darla screamed, as Duncan tried to push past me to get to her on the other side of the bed, but I stood my ground and held onto his machete arm.

"Look at your son, Duncan!" I screamed. "Look at him! Can I pick him up, please? He's got blood on his . . ." I couldn't say it.

"Yeah, why not, if it stops the piece of rag crying," Duncan replied swiftly. I had a feeling his son's screams were doing something to his brain – not a *good* something.

"Thank you," I said, and looked at Darla, willing her to keep her mouth shut for once. Each time the height of drama she called me to witness fell, she did her best to hike it up again. Why did she do that! *Real life* drama wasn't something I was good at.

"See, this is what I tell you about Darla, Anne!" Duncan shouted. I felt his cutlass arm move involuntarily towards her. I knew that if he really wanted to let rip, my hold wasn't strong enough to stop him.

"She is a no-good mother. Which mother would leave their weeks-old baby crying like that?"

Darla's aggressive behaviour with Duncan always left me stumped. Maybe her name-calling was the only way she had of fighting back, using the mouth he had deformed from constant blows, repeatedly ripping her lips open and knocking out her teeth.

I dropped Duncan's arm, picked up Richard and held him close to my heart. The quickened pace of his heartbeat reminded me that, not long ago, *I* was a lonely child like him. With his little bloodied head, Richard searched my chest for food he thought was there, and I moved his head slightly to the middle of my body. His cries were low and weak. He needed his mother, and the milk *she* could give him.

"What's this about, guys?" I asked, holding back the tears I would later shed for the child I held in my arms, and for the one I used to be. I reached out and took the cutlass from Duncan's hand, now that he had relaxed a bit.

"What have I told you about all the mess in this room?" Duncan shouted. "Anne, ask her what I've told her time and time again about the mess. Ask her!"

"Anne, he . . . !" Darla shouted, before I could begin.

"See this is what I talk about," Duncan said calmly, turning to me. "She's so ignorant, she can't even speak. She *shouts*. All she does is shout in my head. I can't take it, Anne. Tell her to go! I want her out!"

"Darla," I said, "Maybe you should spend the night at your Mum's. You know, let everyone have a chance to think and settle down – calm down."

"But Anne, he only tell you his side . . ." Darla began.

"Yeah, this is good! Let's hear your side, man!" Duncan shouted, and Richard jumped in my arms, still whimpering softly, still searching for food from my body.

"You stupid fool, ah talkin'!" Darla shouted back.

I saw the movement in Duncan's eyes and knew he was thinking of snatching the cutlass from me. I threw it under the bed, where it got stuck on something, and grabbed him by the hand. My fingers swiped the rough calluses on his palm, and surprisingly, he didn't pull away.

"Right," I said to Duncan. "I'm taking Darla and Richard over to ours. You stay here and calm down."

At home, while she fed Richard from her dry breasts, I was able to look at the slices in her arm. She riled on about Duncan through the old cuts on her lips. A couple of them seemed infected and seeping. I felt the cold shudder of fear climb up my spine, and wondered where it was when I needed it to *prevent* me from acting like a mad woman.

Mum tells me not to get so involved, because Duncan, in his madness may hurt me too. But he never has, and the mild threat is worth it if it meant I could help Darla.

Mum and I cleaned her wounds, and I preached to her like I always did. I said how terrible it would be for little Richard to grow up always being scared; how little hope a child has when it can't depend on its own skin to always be there to protect its body. Finally, I told her that I *should* be like her.

"Why?" she asked, cradling the baby to her chequered breast. Duncan has been cutting her there too.

"If you know my past, Darla, I should have no self-esteem. I should be in someone's back bedroom being beaten within an inch of my life. Darla, if it's possible for one, it's possible for *anyone.*

"But not everyone's like you, Anne," Darla answered, through her many missing, knocked out teeth. "Not everyone wanna be alone."

"You always say I'm alone, Darla. I have work, and friends, and *family*. And for the first time in my life – gosh, in my grandmother's life – I'm saving a little money! Being with someone should enrich you, not break you up."

But Darla wasn't going to leave Duncan. She would stay with him until she died a 'suspicious' death.

CHAPTER 40 – REFLECTIONS, REFLECTIONS

When I started to hear my name on the office radio, I knew that sooner or later, I would get a call from Razor. By the time it came, everyone in my town who didn't *already* know who I was, knew my name. The dedications came few and far between, but soon I was getting four or five every day.

He called the General Foreman's secretary, the only private number he could find of the mines. The young secretary, the most well-dressed, well-paid woman in the department, sailed into Payroll in her clip, clip high-heels. No one was mad enough to expect *her* to wear the standard issue, flat steel-tipped shoes.

"You'll never guess who just ring me up!" she cried. By the time we walked back to her office she'd made me promise to get a request played for her on the radio.

"I miss you," Razor said, "Just visit me."

Since I no longer worked at weekends, I agreed to travel up to the city on Friday afternoon after work. I suppose if Mum had said not to go, I wouldn't have, but I had gotten so used to making all the decisions for my little family, earning our living, paying our bills and sending my sister to school. I had *forgotten* how to ask for help. Besides, I knew he still needed me to save him.

"I'm a changed man," he said.

"Really?"

"Yes. I've really worked on all the jealousy and bad habits and everything."

"I'll have to see to believe it," I answered.

"Exactly!" he said. "Give me the time it will take for you to see it."

When no persuasive tactic enticed me to leave my job and move back to the city, he moped for a bit, then gave up trying. I travelled back and forth every other weekend, two to three hours each way.

The hours spent travelling and waiting for the ferry turned up many confusing thoughts and deep reflections for me:

In many ways, I still felt like I owned part of the house and was responsible for its beauty. Going back made me feel vindicated in a bizarre sort of way. It made me feel proud that life had made me strong enough to withstand the temptation of living there on a full-time basis.

But what was there to feel so proud of? When did 'being poor' become a badge of honour? When one's life is lacking the very virtue that would make one whole, does being poor become a type of medal one can wear in place of what is truly important for human completeness?

Isn't this switch around a representation of what we have reduced human nature to? Have we ever been able to explain the workings of the eye or how it was made? How does it see without looking? When a person wears glasses, he cannot see properly unless he looks *through* the lenses.

How does the eye *automatically* 'see' without help? Does this ability make the eye greater than the man who can't explain how it does what it is made to do?

I didn't *make* myself poor and can't take responsibility or credit for it. In the same way, the brilliance of my eye cannot give me reason to be proud. After all, I can't explain how it came to be.

By man's explanation, by itself, the eye decided what it was going to do, then took steps to achieve its plan. If it didn't take someone *greater* than the eye to make it, why can't humans make *one* seeing eye?

Even though I can't take responsibility for the eye, I can be a good steward of it. I can nurture it by treating it right, in order to have good sight when I'm old (all things being equal).

I have to treat my circumstances in the same way; work around, and *with* them to try to change the outcome of the things that were given to me.

I know who put the smell in flowers. I know that they – in their infinite passion for beauty, didn't 'decide' what scent they wanted to have in order to attract specific pollinators. I know that He will give me the scent *I* needed too. I just had to use my *brilliant* eye to see the light through all the haze.

After a few weeks, Razor – as he liked to say – now the *potential* Minister of Culture, was invited to a formal dinner.

I was thrilled, but nagging in the back of my mind, I knew this was the acid test. Would I be accused of making too much eye contact with the Prime Minister? With the Minister's aide? How much eye contact is too much?

Instead of being excited, I was worried all week. By Friday night when I got back to the house and had dinner done, I hoped to fall ill so I didn't have to go.

On Saturday, I did my hair carefully, to make it as bland and as simple as possible. I took a blob of Razor's Brylcream into my palms and rubbed it into my hair. The shiny, gold colour it turned – from spending so much time in sunshine, looked darker when oiled or wet.

I deliberated wearing the belt on the new shimmering black dress he'd bought me, but since the front of it was a wrap, the belt it came with *just* had to be worn.

I smoothened my eyebrows with my fingers and rubbed a bit of Vaseline on my lips. My face was done.

I stepped into the black, three-inch-heeled shoes that came with the dress, which now made me over six-foot tall. I realised that no matter *what* I did, I would stand out tonight. Most of the *men* there would be shorter than me, let alone the women. But Razor had changed, hadn't he? He said he had. We would certainly see tonight.

The Minister sat at the head of the table and I was placed not far from him. He and I were the tallest in the room. His silver hair glistened in the low lights, and he almost looked like a majestic angel with a circle of silver halo on the top of his head.

A few large golden birds lay in the middle of the grand table and as we started to eat, a happy din filled the room. I felt wonderfully happy and free, more liberated than I had felt during all the time I spent with Razor in the past. But by dessert, I knew I wasn't going home that way.

I knew that the drive home, with a slightly tipsy Razor at the wheel, would be all and maybe more of what I dreaded. Razor was as far from Duncan as he could be, so why did I feel as unhappy as Darla looked?

"You look very beautiful as always," is what the Minister had said to me. He was Razor's friend. Surely, he meant no offence. Or maybe the offence was rather in my answer of, "Thank you."

Beside Razor in the car, I looked over and studied his face, slack and fallen with the amount of alcohol he'd consumed.

With him, I lied and kept secrets. I didn't like that version of me, the version that nothing else and no one else brought out.

I thought to the future of the life I knew awaited me, of the children I knew I wanted to bear and realised that if I didn't get out of this soon – for good, my kids would have no better life than I did, richer, but no better.

What then would be the purpose of my resolutions to be good? What would be my reward for living my life in the shadow of all the sacrifices I have made, and all the promises I've kept? What would be the drive behind all the times I have abstained from going down the very path my earlier life promised to lead me? What would be the point in all of that? Certainly not this. *Please* God not this.

CHAPTER 41 – LEROY'S FIGHT

"Tho, what yuh going to do 'bout it?" A very edgy Leroy bawled down the street, his lisp was very pronounced in his excited state.

"Yuh want to come and tek me on! Come if yuh 'sink yuh big and throng enough!"

"Yuh frighten!" Izzy screamed back. "Yuh frighten, yuh big pouf!"

"Ah gon thrip you naked thith day!" Leroy screamed. "Yuh doan know me!"

My play had wrapped that evening. It was yet another leading role, yet another promise of payment I knew would never materialise.

"We'd be rich if yuh got paid for all the acting you do," Mum had said to me, and she was right, but I expected that.

We understood, when we took roles in any art form that people were poor and in order to get *any* support at all, tickets had to be cheap enough. But we kept on anyhow. We suffered for our art. Our producers profited off our talents, and some of us got nothing, yet we struggled on.

Leroy had his eye on Izzy, a little, mousey ship girl. Until he turned into a raisin and died of the mystery illness that made him one with his bed, Leroy was big, healthy and strong.

Izzy had stolen one of his men and he wasn't letting her get away with that.

"Ah gon tear yuh eyes out, yuh big antiman!" Izzy spat in Leroy's direction.

No one, no one called Leroy an *antiman*. That was for the little boys in the street not yet in touch with *anyone's* sexuality let alone their own.

Leroy double clicked his fingers in the air shouting, "Girl, ah gon get you good!"

No one saw him move but he was through the barrier of the many people standing in the street and pulling Izzy's long red wig (I *always* thought her hair was too thick – and red, to be real) off her head in a flash. The fight was on.

"Hello, Sunshine!" I heard behind me. Like us, Jerry Saunders only stayed to see the fights if he was in the street when they broke. Since the 'incident' with the tape, I've avoided speaking to him, but living so close to each other made that quite a feat, especially since I'd told no one about what he tried to do to me.

He had taken to calling me Sunshine. One day when I asked him why he had said, "Because the street brightens up whenever yuh walk by."

I was certain he was using compliments to get me up to his room under some *other* pretext. I didn't mind wasting his time.

However, weeks later, when I asked the miners who travelled to work on the bus with us why they called me 'Golden Child,' *they* also said, "Coz you shine things up."

I guessed the opaque membrane that abuse and misery wrapped me in so completely was slowly ebbing away as I grew bigger and bolder, tearing it to shreds.

Perhaps the light that I was given to shine had been so totally hidden, that it had taken this long for me to burst out of my suffocating bondage gauze.

Izzy's wig lay in the gutter like an unwanted, painted rag doll. When the dust cleared, Leroy emerged limping majestically, as only he could, with a split lip. Izzy was lying in the dirt, tugging at her broken bra strap. She made eye-contact with no one as she got up and dragged herself to her makeshift house. At her door, she shouted, "Tonight when Bill (the balding, married insurance salesman they fought over) comes down the street, ah want all'yuh (she swept her arms wide to all of us who were going back to *our* make-shift houses), to watch to see whose door he gon knock at!"

Izzy walked into her house and slammed her door confidently. But the balding, two-timing, three-timing Billy goat stayed away from the street all week and when he finally showed up, Darla, as I corn rowed her hair, told me that he was seeing one of the other ship girls. She (Darla) was expecting baby number two.

CHAPTER 42 – A NEW LIFE

I was at work when the baby finally came. Mum told me that on her way to the market that morning, she had passed Darla sitting on the tiny back veranda holding her tummy.

"Yuh alright, Darla?" she had asked her. Sometime before I started going back to the city, I'd told Darla that if she shouted for Mum when she was in need, that Mum would come. "Don't pay any attention if she fusses," I said. "She'll come anyway."

"Ah think ah having the baby, Auntie Esther."

"We got to go to hospital, then?" Mum asked her.

"No. I got no clothes for the baby," Darla answered. "I shamed to go to the hospital. Yuh know how them nurses are. They gon laugh at me and beat me up."

"So what you gon do, Darla? Yuh can't have the baby here on the steps."

Mum told me that when she said those words, she didn't know that was *exactly* what Darla planned to do. A nurse lived next door to her, right at the front of Miss Bessy's yard. Maybe she figured that if she timed it right, the nurse would be off shift when baby decided to come out.

"Ah got a nurse friend coming over, Auntie Esther. Is alright, you can go," Darla told Mum, and she believed her. It was Mum's turn to learn that even when people made perfect sense, they could be still be lying.

By the time Mum returned with her shopping, Darla was sitting in the same spot, now wet, with a tiny head peeping out of her body.

Mum dropped her shopping and ran over to get the nurse next door. Luckily, she was home sleeping off last night's shift.

It took Mum five minutes of banging on her front door, to wake nursie out of bed.

Little Leah was delivered – her umbilical cord cut with our kitchen knife – then wrapped in our towel.

Mum and the nurse quickly made nappies out of our old sheet.

Darla's plan had worked perfectly. 'Aunty Esther' was on call, and so was the nurse next door. In spite of Duncan's attempts at a termination (by regular punches to her tummy) Darla had delivered a crying, healthy, but tiny baby girl.

By the time Leah was two months old, Darla was pregnant again, so she sent Richard away to stay with her sister and *her* boyfriend who lived across the river.

But before he left, there was enough time for Richard to watch a game of street cricket. I never played, but I watched, holding Richard.

For me, playing street cricket meant that I'd conformed to the street. I was party to its child abusers and baby-breakers who half killed their stepchildren and were allowed to graze freely.

I was scared of having fun with them, wallowing in the lair to which unfaithful husbands slunk under the sheet of darkness.

I never wanted to belong to the lonely place where an old woman gives up her house in order to live her life in peace, and to the haven to which liars, drunks and criminals came to satiate their depraved gluttony.

I never played the street cricket because some day, I will uproot my little family and flee. I will save my sister from the decadence.

A Guyanese Proverb: Wen yuh gat bad luck, wet paper self a cut yuh.

Translation: At a time when you're having particularly bad luck, even wet paper will cut you.

Meaning: When you're at a low point in your life, even minor things will deeply affect you.

CHAPTER 43 – RICHARD IS BACK

I saw him on Sunday evening after I returned from a show. It had been nine months since Darla sent him away to live with her sister, enough time to have a third baby – another little girl. She brought Richard over for me to see him, so that she could have me witness what her sister and her husband had done to him. What greeted me was a sight I hope to never see again.

Richard had never been a chubby boy. He didn't eat well enough for that, but he always had a bit of flesh and smooth black skin that covered all of it, most of the time.

The boy that stood in front of me was a skeleton. The depressed hole in his forehead looked like someone had tucked a drinking straw into it and sucked out a small portion of his skull.

His bottom stuck out. There was hardly any skin left on it, from the amount of beating he'd sustained. The bones protruded like fans on each side of his spine.

Richard reminded me of a stray dog I'd once seen, most of its skin and part of its ears were gone. Its tail – what was left of it, was tucked between its hind legs and it did nothing. When I had made a kissing sound to call it over to where I stood, it stood glued to its original spot and did nothing, moved nothing. It didn't even blink.

Richard stood as still as the dog, as naked as he was born. He was not a child. Man! He was not even a *person* any more. Whatever they'd done to him, it had incised his soul and left an empty shell. Richard was a stick man a child had drawn, then scrapped because it was too blotched. What made me cry was not that they had allowed the hole they made in his head to be eaten away so badly, it seemed the parasites had started munching on the bone. The thing that made me cry was the way he looked at me, staring through my head as though he was waiting for me to hit him.

He looked fifty years old. Wrinkles formed on his partly skinless forehead, on his thighs, and around his mouth, where all his young flesh had fallen away from lack of food.

"Big Man (her sister's boyfriend) beat he, Anne. He beat he bad," Darla repeated. But I could *see* that. The physical abuse was *not* the worst thing he had done to him. I was sure of that.

"Big Man locked Richard in a dark room and starve he for days. Then he take off his clothes and put salt and pepper in all them cuts he make on he skin."

Why didn't your sister do anything, Darla?" I said through grinding teeth. "How could she sit and watch her monster do this to a little boy!" I knew that if Big Man was standing in front of me right then, I would hurt him.

"She frighten bad, Anne. Is what she tell me."

I kept my eyes on Richard, but he stood naked, doing nothing, saying nothing, not even moving – hardly breathing even. They didn't allow him to speak, not even to cry and ask them to stop beating him. The front of his entire body looked like it had been scalded at some time in the past. I knew what a healed scald looked like. I had my own fingers as reference. I noted that the scalding was done when he was as naked as he was in front of me.

I felt guilty for naming him, as if by giving him a name, I had made him this little person, who had suffered more than he could understand.

"Why didn't your sister send him back if they didn't want him!" I shouted. And for the first time, I hated Darla with so much force, I wanted Duncan to punish her.

"She say that Big Man think that Richard is a bad boy and he gon make him straight."

"But couldn't she send you a message to come and pick him up?" I asked, "Before he did all this to your son?"

"She say she scared of Big Man. If she do anything, he gon murder she," Darla answered.

"So it's better for him to murder her nephew?"

"Anne, you don't know Big . . ."
"I don't care, Darla! Look at him! Look at him! I screamed. "You can't *defend* her. Look at the hole in his head!"

"She say that Big Man beat Richard with a hammer and then lock he in the toilet for one whole day. And when Richard cry, Big Man do even worse things."

"Don't tell me that, please," I begged. But why was I being so selfish, I wanted to be spared the pain of what had happened to Richard, but what about *Richard*? He was never going to be spared, was he?

"We have to take him to hospital. He has to get help," I said suddenly, trying to hide my selfishness and the rod which had been put through my heart.

"Look," Darla said simply. She turned him around and pointed to the area of his bottom where some of the skin was bruised off. There were strange markings under the wound. He was beaten with something we couldn't identify.

I didn't look for long, because I didn't want to be haunted by Richard's torture. I knew that my mind would dwell on his pain, that it would see it over and over again.

"Ah have to go tomorrow. The doctors doan work on a Sunday night," Darla said. *She never took him to hospital.*

After I dressed some of his wounds, I looked at Richard in the eyes but saw nothing, nothing at all. He was like no other child I'd ever seen. He was so far removed from the child *he* used to be. He was still waiting for me to hurt him. He must have forgotten who I was.

I knew that crying (maybe) would help liquidise some of the pain, so while washing his raw, infected skin, I expected him to cry. He didn't.

Had I forgotten that children like us have cried so much that we finally use up all our tears? We learn soon enough that pain is a bad-tasting medicine, which you have to swallow down hard and fast because once it goes down, it can't hurt you or anyone else anymore.

So we keep swallowing and digesting, some of us using it for nourishment for the soul, others, as vomit to spew onto the people standing closest to us.

Richard got better slowly and was soon out in the street playing cricket with the other kids, shouting and fighting with his little sisters and his fourth time pregnant mother.

Every time Darla gave birth, she would bring the baby to me. Even when we moved away she found me so that I could see the other little soul she had brought into the world to live in one bedroom and sleep on a little piece of rag on the floor, and listen to her father beat her mother, some say, to death.

CHAPTER 44 – THE END AND THE BEGINNING

The day I went to the gospel meeting was the beginning of my present life. By then I was twenty-two, working hard, and ready to find meaning, the thing I was looking for maybe all my life.

Just before my baptism, I visited Razor for the last time to tell him I was leaving him for good. "I'm going to be a Christian," I said. "I can't see you anymore. I'm changing my life for the better."

"You're leaving me for God," he said eventually. "At least that gives me peace."

When we parted that evening, I knew that like my decision with Cyril, this was truly the end. The line in the road was bright and sunshiny. I was going to put my foot over it, one, then the other, and was going to look back no more. I waved, then I was gone from his life. And it made me feel good.

Please prophet tell me what you see.

"You know, sometimes, we do find the answers to questions we've asked. The answers aren't always obvious at first, but this by no means lessens their impact when they become clear. In fact, many times, waiting for the answer can make it all the more explosive and meaningful to us. Sometimes the answer is right there, but we can't see it because it's not the one we're looking for. 'Hardship is making me stronger for what?' I

used to say, but if our journey can make us stronger to help even just one other person along the way, then it was worth it."

Jon and I halt our discussion when we hear the front gate slam. Like Andy, he's a good listener.

"Sister Anne, Sister Anne!" Nadia runs up to the doorstep shouting through the open door. I hear her before my eyes can make out her little body in the shadow of the dark, moonless night.

This was not the first time Nadia had come to our house. She has lunch with us daily because her two older sisters live with Mum and me, now that we live in a bigger house and Franc has won a place in a renowned technical college.

But every afternoon after school, Nadia must go home to an abusive father and a depressed mother, who's nursing a disabled baby. When I'd offered to foster the girls, Mum thought I had gone mad. Satie – one of my old primary school friends – and I had built up a renewed friendship.

Not long after that, two of her daughters were living with me as my children, catching up on all the school and homework they missed because of poverty and abuse. Our house is modest but we have enough space and food to share.

At first Satie didn't tell me about Ricki, her partner, and how he beat her and the girls. He was often out of a job, and she, a young woman with four daughters – one of them disabled – had to go out and try to make a living.

Jon had stood up when Nadia ran in. He often made the two to three hours' journey from the city to visit me. We're going to be married, you see.

"Come in, Nadia." I say, guessing what was to come. Her big sisters are tucked up in bed. I hope she'll be quiet and not scare them too much.

"Sister Anne, Daddy put me out and he chop Mummy with the cutlass!" Nadia says, visibly shaky. "Mummy said to run and call yuh."

"Okay," I whisper, putting my finger to my lips. "You stay here. I'll go and see. Did you come here by yourself in the black out?"

"Yeah, but ah run really fast, Sister Anne," Nadia replies.

"Don't go anywhere," I tell her. "You're safe. You believe you're safe here, right?"

Nadia nods. I walk into our kitchen and tell Mum I'm going out for a bit. "To see Satie," I say.

"I'm coming!" Jon says, "It's too dark for you to go on your own."

"Not too dark for a seven-year-old to be out by herself," I whisper.

"How could her parents just leave her outside?" Jon asks angrily. "Poor child must be terrified."

"She's more scared of what's happening indoors than of the dark outside, "I answer.

"If I were seven and got locked outside, I'd scream my head off until Mum or Dad came out. Then I'd scream some more until they got me ice cream or something," he laughs and says to Nadia. She looks up at him, confused.

Jon does not understand that you never do that. You're never allowed to show them you're a real person inside. If they can find where 'you' really are, they know how to hurt you better. You become whatever they want you to be, and whenever they change their mind about the object you'd become used to being, you become something new, whatever suits them, whatever, wherever, just so you don't feel the pain.

As we walk to Satie's house, I tell Jon of the time I walked through the burial ground, something unknown for children to do in our town.

"You know, I wasn't even aware I was doing it because I was so scared of my grandmother. I don't understand it – even now, but I was so scared she was going to die."

"But if she died, wouldn't you've been free of her?" Jon asks.

"True. But I was so scared of her that I felt like if she died, she would give me the beating of my life."

"That doesn't make sense, sweetheart," Jon says, and he's right. But he still doesn't understand. Being scared is not about making sense.

Ten minutes later, we walk up to Satie's hut. Jon's foreign shoes are all sodden. He wasn't prepared for the slush of the squatters' side of town.

"Satie!" I call, outside their door, "Satie!"

From inside I hear the muffled sound of her voice. She sounds like she's trying to scream behind something pressed against her mouth.

"Ricki!" I say, "I just want to tell Satie that I have Nadia and she is fine."

"I didn't send her to call you!" Ricki shouts.

"I know, but I just want you both to know that she is alright. Okay?"

"Go away! This is our private party!" came the reply.

"Let me talk to Satie first!" I shout back. The squatters live close to each other and I hope that someone would hear the exchange and come out to help us. No one does. Jon seems scared. He's clearly not used to this kind of thing.

"I'm going to peep through this hole in the door," I say to Ricki. "You better not be chocking her again. You came over the other day and told me that you wanted the girls back at the end of the month because you've changed. You promised me, Ricki."

"Sister Anne!" Satie shouts, "He put the pillow on me face and hold the cutlass to me neck. He's a monster."

"Ask she wot she did, Sista Anne. Ask she wot she did!" Through the incidental peep-hole, I see him walking towards the door, cutlass in hand.

"I come home from me hard labour for she and the girls. Me hands hurt . . ."

("Obviously not enough," Jon whispers beside me).

"Me hands hurt so bad, and you know wot? Me dinner not ready!" Ricki complains.

"She has no one to help with Mariam," I say. "You said yourself that she was hard work."

"Sista Anne, you doan understand. When a man come home from he hard work, he want he food on the table, mon."

I look at Jon, but I don't expect him to agree. He shakes his head and whispers, "What does he do?"

"He chops sugar cane," I tell him. "And he's got his cutlass in his hand."

"Can I see Satie, please?" I ask loudly. "It's dark and the mosquitoes eatin' me alive." "Wait!" Ricki shouts, heading back from where he came. We wait and listen to the crickets calling to each other. In the background, Ricki and Satie continue to argue in whispers inside their hut.

"So this is what you do," Jon states. "Now I understand. How can you be sure he won't turn his weapon on you?"

"I suppose I can't be sure, but they never do, you know. They never do."

"They're scared of you and that mouth," Jon whispers, smiling.

Sadie steps out into the open air and throws herself into Jon's arms, a man she has never seen before. He steadies her by holding her elbows and we talk in whispers, aware that a dozen ears are listening to us behind their little doors.

As we walked away that night, I didn't know that Jon *wouldn't* be the man I would spend my life with. We would break up and I would meet the man of my past dreams – the one of my forever future.

I was sure that Satie would never leave Ricki, though. It was the life she knew even before she'd met him, and the one she would continue to feed on even when her girls stopped needing her. I couldn't help feeling slightly guilty that she didn't escape like I did, because I knew that my past life was well and truly behind me and that was where it would stay forever.

***

As I went down in de valley to pray,
Studying about dat good old way,
When you shall wear de starry crown,
Good Lord, show me de way.

O sister, let's go down.
Let's go down, come on down.
O sister, let's go down,
Down to de river to pray. *

As I walked down towards the river, Mum (who would make the trek a few days later), my sister, and a small group of people stood nearby looking on. I proudly held my balance, digging my toes into the muddy, slippery riverbank. I'd made the decision and no one could hold me back now. I was facing forward, glancing beside me at the smiling faces, but never looking back.

Someone nearby took my hand. I was too focused to see who.

Let's go down, come on down.

The sun had punched a gap in the silken blue sky above, and was shining down with all his might. There was going to be no rain for the rest of today, for this was the day I was heading down to the river. And I was bringing my sister with me.

(*An old, American 19th century slave hymn)

As a baby, I'd had water poured over my head in a man-made, mock-up called, *'Christening.'*

Now I was walking down to the water, to be *baptised* just as Jesus was. I was heading down to be buried under the water, in the fashion I'd read about in the bible *all dem donkey's years ago*.

Ed was already in the river, covered up to his midriff with the dark, muddy Berbice river water. It made me think of the Barbados trip; how the waist-high water had covered me in no time; how Andy had swooped in and lifted me from certain death into life, fresh-air and *breath!*

Ed stretched out his hand to support me into the river. His hand of support remained extended over the next two years in many ways, while I got used to wearing my brand new skin.

O sister, let's go down,
Down to de river to pray.

Ed, Franc and I had practised a dry run of how the baptism was going to be. He'd shown me how he would support my back with one hand, while he tipped me backwards with the other.

I slowly closed my eyes, took a nice, long, deep-deep breath (it felt good) and held my nose tightly before going under. Beneath the water, I heard the singing from far, far away.

In one swift swoop of a hand, I'd risen out of the water, the old life left buried under the surface. Tears and cloudy water ran down my face as I stepped out to the incline of the dark, muddy bank. When I walked away from the river, I knew my past was flowing away, carried by the currents towards Overwinning, ripping through the river, and belching out to sea.

It would be many years before I learned how to breathe deeply, but at least I was now holding my chest out a bit further, and my head a bit higher.

Down to de river to pray.

Epilogue

I finished this book ten years ago! However, with all the problems I had finding, then firing a publisher for Sunday's Child, I put it down and couldn't bear to look at it again. It made me sick sometimes to even think about it.

As some of you know, I had to ask my publishers for my rights (of Sunday's Child) to be returned to me.

I sincerely want to apologise to you, especially those of you who bought the first book just after it was published. You've had to wait for years to read the sequel and this is all my fault. Please forgive me.

For those of you who've asked, there won't be a third book. I have been blessed with a very good life, which would make for an extremely boring book.

If you're wondering why my husband hasn't appeared in Fair Of Face, it's because he's a very private person and has asked not to. We now have teenaged kids and *they* would be mortified if I mentioned their names, hence only three references were made to them.

We're making a short film of Sunday's Child. Please keep following the Facebook page and I'll let you know when it's out. You can contact me on my site: http://www.getconfidence.net

You can also access my author page on Amazon.

Other titles by this author

How to Raise Kids to be Responsible Adults
How to Really Lose Weight Without Dieting
How to Spend Less
Baby Diaries: A Guide For New Mothers
Sunday's Child
Collection of Short Stories (coming soon)